The Art Of
GIVING

The Art Of
GIVING

LIEZEL NORVAL-KRUGER
AND TINA-MARIÉ MALHERBE
with photography by Robbert Koene

UNIVERSE

CONTENTS

First published in the United States of America in 2003

by UNIVERSE PUBLISHING

A Division of Rizzoli International Publications, Inc.

300 Park Avenue South

New York, NY 10010

2003 2004 2005 2006 2007/ 10 9 8 7 6 5 4 3 2 1

Printed in Singapore

ISBN 0-7893-0889-4

Library of Congress Catalog Control Number:

2002117462

First published in 2001 by NK Publishing, 18 Wargrave Road, Kenilworth, Cape Town, South Africa

Introduction

Giving is an international language. Giving a gift

from heart to heart bears a message beyond words;

it is a gesture of love, friendship, celebration, and

acknowledgment. This book is dedicated to giving and

is based on the tradition of handcrafted, personalized

offerings to which we are returning in our increas-

ingly hurried, desensitized age. Many of the ideas it

offers ask that you contact those powerful, often forgotten, emotive wonders – the senses – and give gifts

that awaken others to the joy of the present moment.

Each section will inspire with careful instruction and

inspiration, and supporting recipes, templates, and

do-it-yourself (DYI) explanations to ensure

an effortless creative journey. It will restore your

awareness of the abundance around you, the beauty

of indulgent rituals, and the simple pleasure of

capturing a moment for those you love to experience.

sunday morning snuggling

sensual comfort

sumptuous cushion covers

crisp, laundered linen

tactile, sparkly accessories

covered in supple leather

better for tickling

nesting rituals

soft feathers

contact, caress, suggest

hug closely

suede, satin, silk

sublimely soft

hands that hold

small pleasures

fluffy treasures

relaxation

TOUCH

BEADED COASTERS

These tactile, sparkly accessories are just the thing
for a table's evening dress. Present in a simple bag
made from fine, semi-opaque cloth.
DIY instructions, page 124.

BEAD BOX

Tinkering with beads is both creative and calming –
busy hands free the mind and soothe the spirit. In
less enlightened times, female novelists would often
hide their writing behind handicrafts, surreptitiously
penning their thoughts in between threading and
stitching. Fill a sewing box with a selection of fun
beads, threads, and fastenings and give it to a budding
novelist or anyone seeking inspiration.

SILKY BAG

Make a basic bag from textured, silky fabric and give
it away with a cluster of bright incense sticks.

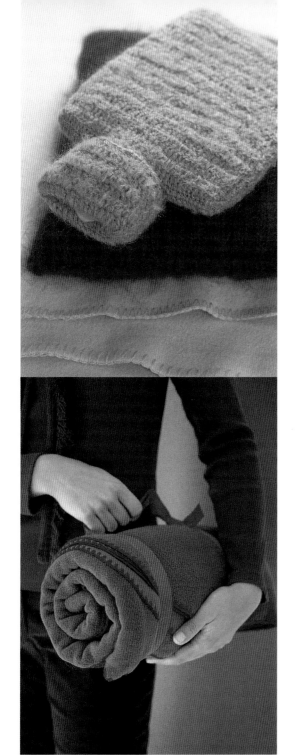

CUP WARMERS

Keep both hands and hot drinks warm with crocheted cup covers. Give them away with a selection of jasmine, ginger, vanilla, peppermint, and coconut teas.

SMALL PLEASURES

Not only cosy, warm, and sensual, a knitted cushion is also a stylish accessory. Conjure up childhood cheer with a crocheted hot water bottle cover to take to bed.

FLEECE BLANKET

Nurturing fabrics play an important part in the nesting ritual – they should be as sublimely soft as possible. Trim a plush piece of fleece with an old-world blanket stitch and give to someone who enjoys sleeping in.

LINEN TABLE RUNNERS WITH VELVET TRIM

Cut a 232 cm/91 in by 47 cm/18$^1/_2$ in rectangle from linen. Sew running stitch 0.8 cm/$^3/_8$ in from the edge, along all four sides, to avoid stretching. With wrong side facing, pin and tack the velvet ribbon, right side facing, along the edge, just overlapping the running stitch. Machine stitch and snip the corners of seam allowance. With the right side of the main fabric facing, flap the ribbon and seam allowance over to the right side on all sides (leaving the corners undone) so that the fold of the hem lines up with the outer edge of the ribbon; press lightly and tack along inner edge of ribbon. Mitre and tack the corners. Top-stitch along inner edge of ribbon and finish the corners with slip-stitch.

CUTLERY HOLDER

Make useful table accessories for family and friends like this holder to store and protect a special set of cutlery.
DIY instructions, page 124.

PLACE-MATS

These are best made with a reversible fabric. Cut 57 cm/22$^1/_2$ in by 42 cm/ 16 $^1/_2$ in) rectangles from the fabric. With the fabric right side up, fold over a 1 cm/$^1/_2$ in return on all sides and press. Leaving the return in place, fold over a 5 cm/2 in seam on all sides and press. Unfold the seam and fold in the corners so the diagonal fold aligns with the straight fold lines in the seam. Turn in one seam along the seam line, crease to form a neat corner, press, and tack. Turn in seams on all sides, forming neat corners, press, and tack. Top-stitch hem in place close to the inner edge with matching thread. Use matching embroidery thread to finish the corners with two large cross-stitches.

FRENCH LINEN NAPKINS

Table settings are an important element in creating different dining moods. Beautiful, finely textured linen napkins make any occasion special.
DIY instructions, page 124.

WHITE CHRISTMAS

Create a serene spiritual space for your friends and family at Christmas time. Dried branches sprayed white and silver make striking, sculptural trees while topiaries made from rosemary bushes and hung with small silver balls are wonderfully simple decorations or gifts. A shimmery organza tablecloth will catch the light, casting wonderful textures around the room.

PRETTY PARCELS

Place mini boxes, covered in white and tied with ribbon threaded through dress clips, decorative buckles or brooches, on the table. Spend a few weekend mornings wandering around antique markets looking for your fasteners. For fluffy treasures, wind a thin feather boa around a parcel – it will double up as a scarf or to line cuffs and collars.

WREATHS AROUND GLASSES

Make mini wreaths out of leaves and berries, and place them around the tops of drinking glasses. Finish with a candle or night light. Great to give away as table decorations or to adorn mantelpieces.

DAINTY DECORATIONS

Spend some quality family time making Christmas decorations over tea or a glass of wine. Gather straight twigs from the garden, cut them to size and create celebratory symbols by securing with string. Bend thin wire into a heart shape – string delicate beads onto it and close. Suspend a single crystal bead on the end of embroidery thread in the centre.

PAPER PACKET WITH STARS

Make a basic paper packet, attach stars and close with thin wire. Fill with Christmas decorations, *lebkuchen*, Christmas crackers, paper crowns, candy canes, or other festive trinkets. Basic paper packet template, page 122. Star diagram, page 121.

CHRISTMAS FAIRY

Spoil your little princess with a tutu and tiara ensemble. Use thin wire to make the tiara. First get a basic circle by measuring a little head, then work star and heart shapes into the wire, threading beads as you go. Place them in layers of tissue paper in a round cake tin sprayed light blue, or in a hat box covered in light blue wallpaper or fabric. Decorate with white felt cut-out clouds.

VELVET PIN CUSHION

This makes a delightful sewing companion for a creative friend. Cut two 12 cm/4³/₄ in squares from velvet. Place velvet right sides facing and stitch all sides, leaving a 4 cm/1¹/₂ in gap on one side. Press the seam allowances along the open edge to the wrong side, clip the corners and turn right side out, pushing corners out carefully with a blunt knitting needle. Fill with a polyester fiber filler of your choice and stitch to close. To make the hanging loop of beads: starting on one corner, make a large knot in a double thread (use strong polyester thread) and pass the needle through one corner of the pin cushion. Thread the beads on and pass the needle back through the fabric, finishing off with a few tiny stitches.

COLOR CODED

Fill the kit with the usual essentials and be sure to keep the colors in your loved one's wardrobe in mind when selecting cotton.

SEWING KIT

Use two beautiful fabrics, like tactile felt and crisp taffeta, to make a little sewing kit for emergencies or to take along on travels.
DIY instructions, page 125.

ORGANZA SHOEBAG

The ultimate gift for a friend with a shoe fetish. Cut one 84 cm/33¹/₂ in by 35 cm/14 in rectangle from the main fabric. Cut a 45 cm/18 in piece of cord. Fold the fabric in half, with right sides facing; pin, tack and machine stitch one of the long sides for 36 cm/14¹/₂ in, leaving 6 cm/2¹/₄ in unstitched at the top. Machine stitch a continuous line on the other long side. Fold the top raw edge 1 cm/¹/₂ in over to the wrong side all around and press. Fold over a further 5 cm/2 in, lining up the side seams. Press, pin, and tack in position. Machine stitch all around the top of the bag 3 cm/1¹/₄ in from the folded edge. Make a second row of stitching 2 cm/³/₄ in below the first row. Turn through and press. Attach a safety pin to one end of the cord and guide it through the casement hole. Remove the safety pin and tie the ends of the cord together into a single knot. Pull the cord to draw. If working with sheer or lightweight fabric make neat, tiny French seams that look good from both sides and hide the raw edge within the seam. For a more decorative finish, consider fell seams.

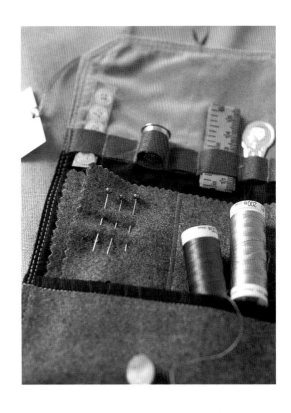

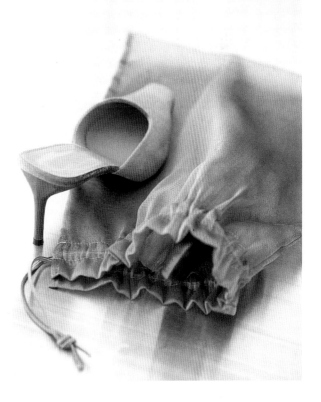

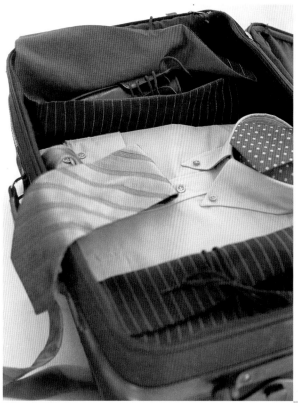

PINSTRIPE SHOEBAGS

Make a smart bag for his all-occasion shoes. Cut 57 cm/22$\frac{1}{2}$ in by 39 cm/15$\frac{1}{2}$ in rectangles from the main fabric and lining. Place the main fabric and lining right sides together, and stitch all sides leaving a gap on one short side. Lightly press the seam allowances along the open edge to the wrong side, trim the seams, clip the corners, and turn right side out, pushing corners out carefully with closed scissors. Press well and stitch to close. Top-stitch along the edge of one of the short sides, fold over 19 cm/7$\frac{1}{2}$in to the lining side and pin and tack side seams to make a pocket. Top-stitch along the edge of the two long sides and one short side (but not the bottom edge of the pocket – the folded edge). Reinforce the pocket seams with a second top-stitch. Insert shoes, fold over flap and tie with a shoelace to close.

BUNCH OF GUINEA FOWL FEATHERS

Tie a bunch of soft feathers up in ribbon and present them to your lover. Look out for them on walks in the country, especially along paths you may have wandered together to give the gift added romance. They look magical among fresh flowers but are even better for tickling. Pack a little massage oil in your pocket and suggest a soothing foot massage. Win her over by ending with feather strokes all over her soles.

COVERED NOTEBOOKS

Transform plain notebooks by covering them in fabric.
For the poet, write out a favorite poem in the front of the book.
For the traveller, get hold of sentimental fabric – like his grandpa's suit material – to comfort while away.
For the journal keeper, cover in leather and have his name embossed on one of the edges.
For the dreamer, write a list of dream symbols at the back of the book for quick referencing.
Hand them over with a beautiful pen or an antique ink well.

SCATTER CUSHIONS

Make sumptuous cushion covers by combining contrasting textures like felt and satin. To make the pad: cut two pieces of lining for each cushion.
Place right sides together and stitch all sides leaving a small gap on one short side. Turn right side out.
Fill the bag with feather down or a polyester fiber filler of your choice and stitch to close. To make the cover: cut rectangles of felt and silk. Cut an additional rectangle of silk for cushions using felt with a cut-out pattern. Place felt and silk with right sides together and stitch all sides, leaving a gap on one short side. Press the seam allowances along the open edge to the wrong side, clip the corners and turn right side out, pushing corners out carefully with closed scissors. If using felt with a cut-out pattern, place the right side of the silk on wrong side of felt and tack to hold fabric in place. Place the felt side, right sides together, with the second piece of silk and proceed in the same way as step two. Insert the cushion pad, making sure that all four corners are well tucked into the cover. Slip-stitch the opening together. The seam will have to be unpicked and resewn for cleaning.

PHOTO ALBUM COVERED IN SUEDE

Buy a basic photo album and cover in two-tone
mock suede. Cut the endpapers at the spine to
loosen the case cover, envelop in suede and attach
to the body of the album with new endpapers. Have
this done professionally at a book binders if you prefer.

OFFICE STORAGE

Transform a sectional container into stylish office
storage space. Spray the lid silver and fill with useful
desktop accessories.

PHOTO MOUSE PAD

Put a picture of someone special on a mouse pad
as an alternative to a framed photo. Take a
photograph to your local digital imager.

COVERED NOTEBOOK

Photocopy a lovely image and fold to slip over an
everyday notebook.

COVERED FRAMES

Buy inexpensive, flat wooden frames in a
contemporary shape and cover in a fabric of
your choice. Velvet, mock suede, tweed, and silk
are exquisite options.

CHINESE SILK FILOFAX

Make checking the diary a momentary luxury during
a busy day. Run up a loose slip cover for a standard
diary in luxurious Chinese woven silk or a special
piece of antique fabric.

FINGER PUPPETS

Inspire budding performers with finger puppets from your local toy shop or craft market. Wrap them in bright packets and fasten with pipe cleaners.

BEANBAGS

Beanbags are an excellent developmental toy. Use them in games of catch to develop hand-eye co-ordination – they're soft, so they won't do any harm and heavy enough to catch easily. Soft textures are also very comforting so use felt and cross-stitch a fun figure applique onto the front. Fill them with assorted types of beans for different textures and weights.

PLAY DOUGH

Make play dough for hours of therapeutic fun with:
300 g/10 oz flour
180 g/7 oz salt
30 ml/2 tbsp cream of tartar
3 ml/less than a tsp sunflower oil
500 ml/15 fl oz water
5 ml/1 tsp vanilla (optional)
Place all ingredients in a pot, stir continuously and bring to the boil. Boil for three minutes, remove from heat and allow to cool. Divide into balls, add food coloring of your choice and knead well until even color is achieved. If you prefer, add a few drops of essential oil diluted in a carrier oil to stimulate the senses. Lavender or camomile to calm; rosemary to uplift, and lemon to sharpen concentration. Check safe quantities with your aromatherapist.

POUCH SURPRISES

Look out for fun, feely bags and fill them with dinky toys and treats.

LIFESAVER BOATS

Colorful, sweet-filled paper boats make great party favors and children will have fun launching them in the water afterwards.

FISHING NET WITH GOGGLES

Encourage hours of sensory stimulation with beach exploration essentials.

GONE FISHING

Place goggles, flippers and a plastic blow-up fish in a fishing net and wrap up in a bandana. A great introduction to traditional family holidays by the sea.

BAGS OF TOYS

Place plastic sea animals inside a ziplock plastic bag and add some colored water. Thread them onto a bath chain. (Warning: choking hazard, small parts and plastic bag. Not for children under three years.)

ylang ylang and jasmine

sweet vapors

massed foliage

gloriously scented

nature's reward

handmade soaps tempt

breathe in

incorporate heaven

calming rose petals

feelings, mood

sublime slumber

cedar, sage, bay leaves

evocative edge

perfume

sweet-smelling yield

dreamy presence

exotic and heady

sweetpea summer

SMELL

SILK ENVELOPES

Delight the luxury lover with these sexy little French silk envelopes. Fill the inner sachets with dried rose petals scented with jasmine and ylang ylang pot-pourri oils. Embroider a message on the inner sachet or slip a handmade card between the folds. Tie a bunch together with a gorgeous ribbon or place them between layers of colored tissue paper in a box. Great for lingerie drawers or jewelry.

SWEET DREAMS

Lavender is the perfect sleeping companion as its relaxing properties encourage serenity, gentleness, and emotional balance. It's also said to incorporate heavenly energies into the physical, so be an angel and fill feminine organza pouches with dried lavender, put them into a bowl and hand them out at the end of a dinner party. Cut 18 cm/7 1/4 in organza squares, place a tablespoon of lavender in the center, bring the corners together, and use a satin ribbon or cord to close. Have a "sweet dreams" stamp made, or use a stencil or a computer to generate your message. Photocopy this label, page 121.

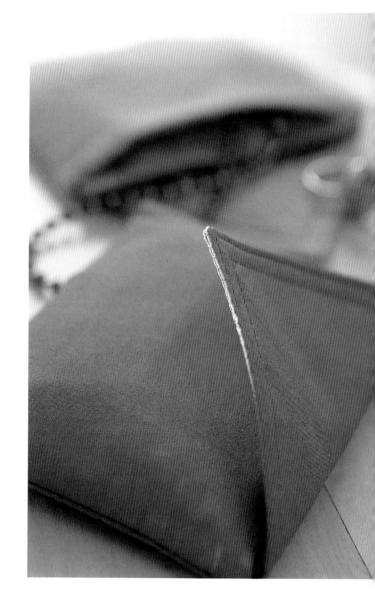

LINEN SPRAY

For sublime slumber, mix one part rose water with two parts water, pour into a bottle, and spritz over freshly laundered linen. Make your own by adding 10 drops of rose oil to 100 ml/4 fl oz distilled water and shake well. Alternatively, fill a pan with the petals of home-grown, heavily scented roses. Add just enough water to cover, place a lid over the top and bring to the boil. Leave to cool with the cover on and strain.

BLISSFUL PETALS

Don't let heavily scented garden roses go to waste. Harvest petals, and give away fresh or dried. Fresh petals are great lightly crushed in the bath – dried petals can be used as pot-pourri or to make scented sachets. To dry: spread them over a porous surface (mesh or a strainer) to aid ventilation, leave to dry, and add a few drops of rose pot-pourri oil.

BUNCH OF ROSES

Choose a flower color according to its vibration. Different colors work within the body's energy field to stimulate certain feelings. Pink evokes feelings of peace and love; yellow, optimism; red, decisiveness and stability. Cleopatra surrounded herself with roses, even lining her bedroom walls with red roses (red stimulates passion). Present these enticing blooms in a folded paper pouch lined with wax paper.

SOOTHING SOAP

Wrap soaps individually and tie with thin wire and a bound rose quartz crystal. Crystals are believed by many to have healing powers; rose quartz is said to calm and to soothe an aching heart. Place one in the bath and allow its nurturing energy to permeate the water for at least 20 minutes, then submerge yourself and let the love flow.

ROSEPRINT FABRIC BOXES

Cover a few boxes using roseprint, embossed wall-paper, and striped canvas. These romantic containers can be used to store towels or bath products.

ROSE BATH SALT

In a large bowl mix:
400 g/1 lb sea salt crystals
200 g/8 oz baking soda
10 drops rose essential oil
10 drops ylang ylang essential oil
10 drops sandalwood essential oil

Throw in some dried rose petals and store in an airtight container.

Salt is a powerful addition to any bath as it draws out toxins and smoothes the skin. Essential oils evoke feelings through smell and restore well-being. Rose will uplift and calm, sandalwood relieves anxiety, and ylang ylang inspires confidence and seduction. Remember that essential oils are potent and should always be used with care. Avoid using them during pregnancy.

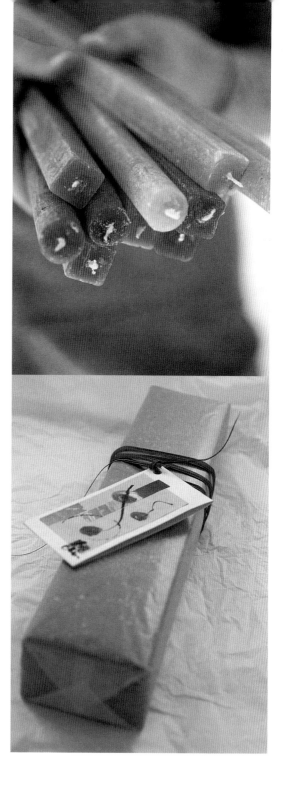

HEAVENLY INCENSE

Incense has long been enjoyed in homes for its evocative edge and dreamy presence. Make a careful selection, some exotic and heady, some light, depending on where they'll be used, and give them away in shimmery organza pouches. To make: cut rectangles of organza, leaving a 2 cm/3/4 in seam allowance on the top edge and 1 cm/1/2 in along the side and bottom edges. Fold over 1 cm/1/2 in onto the wrong side across the top edge of one of the short sides of the rectangle, fold over again to the same width to create a double hem, pin, and machine stitch. Bring the two long sections together with the wrong side facing and machine stitch a 5 mm/1/4 in seam along the entire length. Snip the seams at the corners and turn through (with right sides facing), machine stitch along the entire length to form a roll seam, turn right side out, and press. Place incense inside the pouch and close with a metal or satin cord.

SCENTED CANDLES

Candlelight embraces space in a gentle, flickering glow, it silences a busy mind, and is said to enhance the chi in a room. Wrap scented candles in richly colored wax paper, bind with raffia, and spritz lightly with water to create a mottled effect. Each scent evokes a different mood so consider lifestyle, challenges, desires or new events in the lives of those you're buying for. If love is in the air, jasmine will help it along; if they're studying, rosemary will keep them alert; sadness calls for bergamot, and spoiling for vanilla.

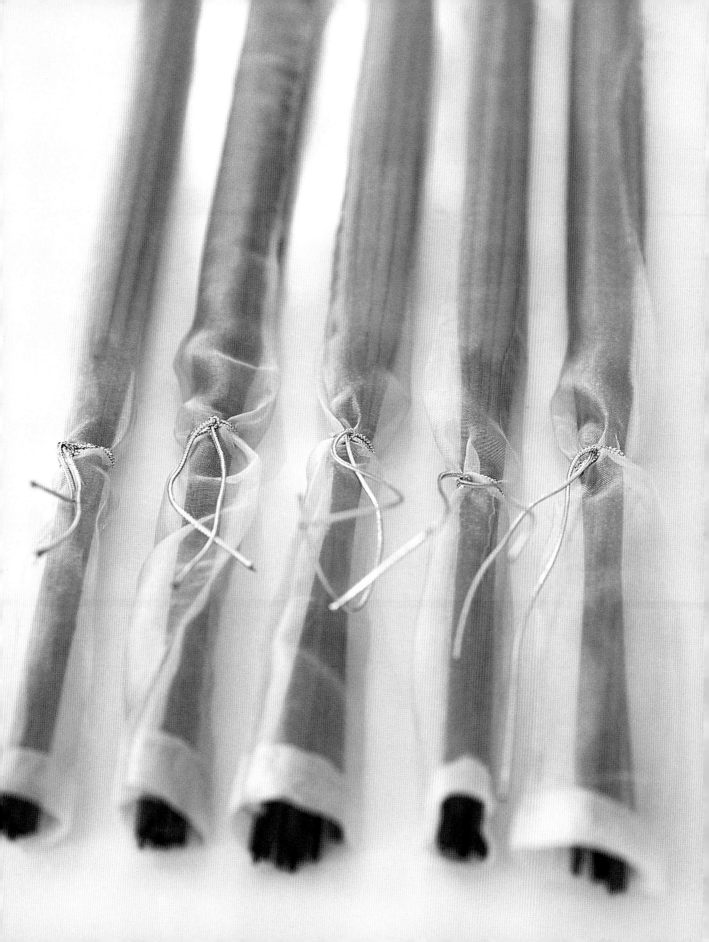

FLOWER BOX

Line a white box with cellophane, cut Oasis to size, soak and arrange rosebuds so their faces greet your loved one as the box is opened. Place embroidery thread and a small card around the lid.

ROSES ON A BED OF GRASS

Cut Oasis into a square, soak in water and pack in slightly opened rosebuds on five sides. Cut pieces of wheatgrass with shears and place on a tile or piece of slate, put the roses on top and finish with thin copper thread and a card.

ROSES WITH CELERY STICKS

Cover an old tin with celery sticks cut to length and tie with raffia. Cut Oasis to size and soak for one hour. Arrange full roses so their heads escape over the rim.

SINGLE BLOOMS

Use single blooms to adorn your gift of glassware. Present them on a tray or packed in an open box.

MINI GARDEN

Lime wash a wooden container. Trim the sides of a tray of wheatgrass, leaving a little tuft in the middle, and place it in the centre of the container. Put damp Oasis along the sides, arrange simple flowers symmetrically and fill in the gaps with pebbles.

RAMBLING ROSE

Indulge a green-fingered genius with these pruned rose bushes which need to be planted on the spot. Dedicated growers around the world spend years creating new varieties of rose, so there are many gloriously scented hybrids to choose from. The rose is also seen as the jewel in any aromatherapist's collection of scented oils as it's profoundly feminine scent promotes balance and joy. Add a card to your gift with a picture of the blooms that'll eventually appear.

FRAGRANT SEEDLINGS

These little ones look super sweet in individual cups presented on a wooden tray, and they smell delightful too.

GIFTS FOR THE GARDEN

There are few things as satisfying as tending a garden, even if it's only on the balcony. Planting seeds with the promise of a bright, sweet-smelling yield; watching the delicate shoots rising from the soil and the buds slowly forming. If your friends have a small garden or are setting up house, sweetpea seeds attached to a planting pot will help them feel at home. Their charming flowers and sweet scent signal the start of summer, a lovely symbol of new beginnings.

NATURE'S REWARD

Great for the gardening novice: alyssum grows abundantly without the expert's touch.

WHITE SCENTED HEART

Fill a linen heart with the fragrance of your choice. This can be hung on a coat hanger to gently scent someone's shirts, placed at the foot or on the headboard of a bed or hooked over a dressing-table chair.
DIY instructions and template, page 125.

EMBROIDERED SACHETS

Turn pieces of scrap material into a selection of scented sachets with embroidered motifs.

MOTH CHASERS

Make natural moth repellents to save clothes. Cut rectangles from natural materials like cotton or linen, fold in half lengthwise, right sides facing, pin and machine stitch the two long sides, leaving the top edge raw, turn through and fill with cedarwood, sage, or bay leaves. Tie a cord around the top to close, and add a label.

TRAVEL KIT

Prepare a practical travel kit to keep high-flying friends washed and groomed for the long haul. Vacuum pack unisex essentials in the way you would food for the freezer, by sucking the air out of a plastic bag through a straw. Include a toothbrush, toothpaste, comb, moisturizer, face splash, foot bath, and facecloth – and close with cardboard and a male/female symbol. Color photocopy this symbol, page 121.

BATHING BEAUTY

Bathrooms are centers of calm and restoration, where we immerse in precious water, contact our bodies, and clear our minds. Aid this indulgence by fine tuning a few bathroom essentials. The sight of cleanly packaged products and the prospect of a sojourn within their vapors is enough to tantalize tiredness away. "Good enough to eat" bath products like food-flavored soaps, keep-in-the-fridge products and culinary packaging add a new dimension to this sensory experience. Fill jars with salts, bath bombs, or handmade soaps and make your own sachets by placing two heaped teaspoons of bath salts onto the middle of a gauze square (found at most pharmacies), bring the corners together, tightly wind thread around the top and end with a double knot. Hang an engraved metal dog tag around the neck of the jar. These can be bought in different colors and metals at pet stores and engraved at jewelers. For more foody bath treats, wrap chunks of milky soap in tracing paper bearing the soap's name and place them in a plastic netting bag once used to carry oranges, or cut soap to the dimensions of a standard packet of butter and imitate the folds of real butter packaging by wrapping in a double layer of white and wax paper, and paste a simple logo onto the side. Suggest lashings all over.
Color photocopy the butter label, page 121.

PRETTY FEET

Present fresh-feet foot bath oil (see below) in a small essential oil bottle and add a label to identify the blend of oils.
Photocopy the label, page 121.

SOLE FOOD

Put this foot spa together for those on their feet all day. Reflexologists believe that the body's internal organs have corresponding nerve centers in the feet, which, when stimulated, can dispel toxins and promote good health. Just soaking the feet in warm water is a beneficial stress reliever. Collect smooth pebbles, mix oils into fresh-feet foot bath (see recipe below) and tie with an exfoliating cloth to stimulate circulation. Advise a weary friend to place the pebbles in the bottom of a basin, cover with warm water, add a few drops of fresh-feet foot bath and glide feet over the pebbles' surface for a gentle massage.

Fresh-feet foot bath
100 ml/4 fl oz carrier oil (almond oil, for example)
2 drops peppermint oil
2 drops tea tree oil
4 drops sandalwood oil
1 drop menthol oil

The language of flowers was a matter of social discourse in the past, when choice, color, arrangement, and offering were all codes between lovers and friends – girls with too many suitors had merely to turn a hopeful's bouquet upside down to signal complete rejection. They no longer carry such exacting messages, but flowers still communicate and there are few gifts to match their natural abundance and evocative presence.

PEEPING POPPIES

Arrange cut reeds around a slim bottle, and secure around the top and bottom with sisal cord. Trim the reeds at the top to form an uneven edge and finish with a single flower.

SLATE CONTAINERS AND MASSED FOLIAGE

Pack slate or lead containers with fragrant foliage.

NESTLING BLOSSOMS

Scour the countryside in windy weather for fallen bird's nests to hold a precious flower.

CHILL OUT KIT

In Japan, bathing is an art form, where ritual and environment combine to bring serenity and *yudedako* – the equivalent of Nirvana. The body is cleaned before entering the bath using a hand towel, before submerging in scalding water to float and dream. Put together a gift of soap and cloth for a preliminary scrub; mustard bath for a long, hot soak to relieve stress and draw out toxins; and almond oil for a warming after-bath massage. Photocopy the chill out label, page 121. Place the copy face down on a piece of balsa wood. Wipe over the back of the paper with a cloth impregnated with lighter fuel, so that the words transfer across.

SOAP STRAINER

Help to create an optimum bathing environment with an eastern feel. Look around for a simple soap dish and make a soap strainer: cut six pieces of bamboo to the required length with secateurs, place in a criss-cross pattern, and bind with sisal or string.

wonderfully warming

chili favorites

organically grown

cuban with calvados

penetrate the air

decadent deliciousness

liquid warm

flavor, relish, savor

intoxicating potions

sweet aromatic spices

essential, earthly offerings

bites of contentment

vanilla seeds in clotted cream

sublime

luscious

savored over days

sensual preamble

TASTE

ALMOND CHOCOLATE DATES

Dates filled with marzipan and dipped in chocolate, nestling in delicate white paper cases, can be savored one by one. Place them in a white box, seal with a black ribbon and lead a friend into temptation.
Recipe, page 114.

SWIVEL STICKS

Melt 100 g/4 oz of chocolate over hot water in a heat-resistant bowl. Wait for the chocolate to soften and stir until smooth. Dip the sugar sticks into the bowl, shake off the excess, and place on greaseproof paper to dry. Repeat if you desire more chocolate. Part with them if you can.

HOT CHOCOLATE CREAM

Chocolate will bring you closer to most hearts, not just because it tastes incredible but for its ability to prompt the release of feel-good endorphins in the brain. For a decadent drink, add two heaped spoonfuls of chocolate cream to a tall glass and smother in warm milk. You'll need 250 ml/8 fl oz of cream and 200 g/8 oz of chopped dark chocolate to make the chocolate cream. Bring the cream to the boil and remove from heat. Add the chocolate, leave for a few minutes, and stir until the chocolate is smooth. Stir occasionally until cool, pour into a jar and seal. Photocopy this label, page 121.

COATED COFFEE BEANS

A wonderful gift to fuel the weary worker. Fill a choice cup and saucer with chocolate-covered coffee beans for a potent pick-me-up.
*Chocolate is best stored in a cool place, but do not refrigerate.

HEART-SHAPED COOKIE
IN A BAG

Use Vylene to make a see-through bag to hold a large heart-shaped cookie. Don't use expensive materials as the biscuit's buttery residue may spoil it.
Basic biscuit recipe, page 114.

LAVENDER HEARTS

Give a basic biscuit recipe an interesting flavor by adding lavender or other herbs. Place them in a paper bag and sprinkle with the herb's delicate flowers.
Recipe, page 114.

MILK AND HONEY BREAD

A wonderful gift for someone in the throes of setting up a home. Christen their new baking tin with delicious bread and rush over to give a hand.
Recipe, page 115.

PISTACHIO NUT COOKIES

Using a knitting needle or skewer, make small holes in these biscuits before you put them into the oven and give a box of them away to be used as scrumptious threaded decorations. Tie one of the cookies onto your gift to stimulate the tastebuds. You can use this wrapping idea for any box of biscuits, just remember to make a hole in one of them for the packaging.
Recipe, page 115.

COFFEE AND BISCOTTI

Coax your friend or lover into a coffee break. Cover paper cups with white paper bearing a printed message of your choice and pour out two strong, restoring coffees. Fill another cup with gorgeous biscotti and make someone's day. Photocopy this label, page 121. Recipe, page 115.

GRANOLA TO GO

Healthier than a bacon and egg sandwich and delicious too. Make it by volume using a measuring jug. You'll need 60 ml/2 fl oz butter, 60 ml/2 fl oz honey, 5 ml/1 tsp ground cinnamon, 500 ml/2 cups rolled oats, 250 ml/1 cup wheatgerm, 250 ml/1 cup bran cereal, 125 ml/^{1}/2 cup sunflower seeds, 125 ml/^{1}/2 cup sesame seeds, 125 ml/^{1}/2 cup raisins and 125 ml/1 cup chopped dried apricots or other dried fruit and nuts. Lightly brush a large baking tray with vegetable oil. Melt butter, then stir in the honey and cinnamon. In a large bowl, mix all the dry ingredients except dried fruit and nuts with the butter and honey. Spread the mixture onto the tray and bake in a preheated oven at 180°C/350°F/gas 4 for about 30 minutes, turning several times, until golden and dry. Remove from the oven and stir in the raisins, apricots, and nuts.

GRANOLA

LEADER'S LUNCH

Do lunch for those with no free time. A set of steel lunchboxes and a sleek flask has the honed, functional edge busy executives enjoy. Fill the flask with revitalising citrus cooler straight from the freezer (recipe, page 115), write a chipper message on an efficiently recycled suitcase tag, and don't forget the steel tumblers. Look out for stylish packaging to keep food fresh – silver bubble foil for CD postage is good for just that. Make a tasty sandwich for a carbohydrate boost and fill another box with fresh tomatoes for the vitamin intake, a nifty folding fork will help the medicine go down. Tie it all up with packing tape and show your initiative.

AFTER DINNER TREATS

For those who prefer savory treats (and men generally do), wrap up a mini platter of home-baked oatmeal biscuits · (recipe, page 116), kumquat jam, mature cheddar, and camembert. Raffia has a good textured finish for a casual, masculine feel and gingham wax paper will both protect the cheese and add a certain European romance to your gift. Be sure to put the biscuits in a tin to keep them fresh and crunchy. Present this with a silver cheese knife for future use.

CHEF'S APRON

A pleasure to behold and practical too, this long white apron is perfect for the avid cook and his admiring spectators. Add a cooking utensil or two for more encouragement, a good mezza luna or a wonderful set of knives will do, or throw in a good recipe book and set a dinner date.

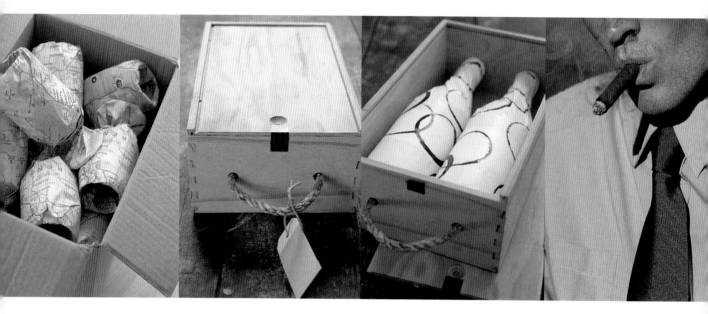

MAP-WRAPPED GLASSES

These make a great house-warming gift. Color photocopy a map of the area your friend has moved to and use pieces to protect and wrap a selection of glassware.

WINE LOVERS

Wrap two bottles in "wine-stained" tissue paper, but use red glass paint instead of wine to stain the paper as the latter will turn brown. Place them in a rustic wooden box.

CHOICE CIGARS

Cigars made a comeback a few years ago, giving the idea of a Cuban with Calvados renewed glamour. Visit a cigar specialist and select a couple on recommendation, wrap in leaves, and tie with sisal string.

ORANGE INFUSED BRANDY

MULLED WINE 1 bottle dry red wine. • 30ml brown... small piece of fresh ginger, peeled and thinly slice... ...i cinnamon stick fr... ...orange. Combine... ...heat but do not boil. Turn down the heat to low an... ...ready to serve. Strain t...

NIGHTCAP

For a calming, night-time drink, add spice-infused teabags (see below) to a saucepan of milk (1 liter/1 quart) and bring to the boil. Add two ceylon teabags and allow to draw for five minutes. Add sugar to taste.

VANILLA SUGAR

Cut a single vanilla pod into short lengths and store it in a jar of sugar. The pod will outlast the sugar so suggest topping up when necessary. The vanilla can even be removed to flavor jams, then washed, dried, and returned to the sugar.

SPICE-INFUSED TEABAGS

Cut gauze or muslin into squares, and hand or machine stitch three sides. Fill each one with three cloves, four cardamon seeds, two cinnamon sticks, and stitch closed. Store in an airtight container.

INFUSED BRANDIES

These are ideal as a thawing drink and are delicious additions to home cooking. Decant brandy into a gift bottle and either add a long cinnamon stick, a vanilla pod, or fresh orange peel. The orange peel brandy will keep for three weeks and the others, for six months.

GLUHWEIN GLOW

Mulled wine has a wonderfully warming taste and aroma and is bound to take the edge off a winter's night. Pour red wine into a lovely old bottle, fold and tie a *gluhwein* recipe over the opening, and attach a bag of the ingredients to complete the set.
Recipe, page 116.

CHEERS!

Serve *gluhwein* in a pretty glass with *panettone* or other cakes and spicy breads.

FLORENTINES

In Germany it is customary to exchange family biscuits at Christmas time to bring glad tidings and joy. Place these festive florentines between layers of wax paper to prevent them from sticking and pack in a long white box.
Recipe, page 116.

LEBKUCHEN

Give these traditional treats away in a cut-out-star paper bag.
Recipe, page 117.
Basic paper packet template, page 122.

NEW STEAM

Overthrow the old Christmas pudding by preparing a delicious lemon dessert in its place.
Recipe, page 117.

HIDDEN DEPTHS

Disguize this new Christmas recruit in white cloth tied with a soft ribbon in traditional red, and make a simple card to attach.

SINFULLY GOOD

Do your dessert duty with decandent servings supported by dollops of lemon curd. Equal parts cream and lemon curd is another powerful secret weapon. Call in the troops.
Recipe, page 117.

TURKISH DELIGHT

Turkish towns are lined with sweet stalls selling unbelievable arrays of these aromatic treats and a languid hour spent acquiring each flavor is a traveller's essential. A British man must have been doing just that when he labelled them Turkish Delight, but their true name is Rahat Lokum, which means "little bite of contentment." These blissful sweets are usually served on birthdays or other special occasions and because they last for up to six months, most Turkish households have them on hand. Allow their soft texture and exotic taste to bring a sigh to someone's lips. Place the pretty bites in a box amid dustings of icing sugar and finish with an organza ribbon.

MINI CAKES

Prepare this gift box for a child or to awaken the child within. Bake or buy a basic sponge cake. Turn it upside down and cut into circles with a cookie cutter. Sieve 200 g/8 oz of icing sugar into a bowl and add 30 ml/2 tbsp of hot water to give it a runny consistency. Spoon the icing onto the center of the cakes and smooth using a palette knife. Place cakes in a box and fill a second box with cake decorations — sweets, little flowers made from icing sugar, small tubs of edible food coloring, shredded coconut mixed with green food coloring to resemble grass, and so on. Tie the two boxes together with bright cord and spell out the recipient's name with threaded alphabet beads. If you decide to make the boxes from scratch, be sure to use non-toxic materials.

BATHING TEDDIES

A charming alternative to the gingerbread man for a little person to snack on. Trace and cut out the card template on page 114. Roll a basic biscuit dough on a floured surface to a 3 mm/^{1}/$_{12}$ in thickness, place the template onto the dough, and cut out the bears using a sharp knife. Place on a baking tray lined with non-stick baking paper and bake in a preheated oven at 220°C/425°F/gas 8 for 10 minutes, or until cooked. Cool, decorate with icing, and place them on a little towel of striped brown paper — use non-toxic crayons to make the stripes. The bears will fit into a standard CD gift box. Basic biscuit recipe, page 114.

TEA

Tea is pause in a busy day, solace, spiritual symbol, a shared ritual. *Cha'* became the Chinese national drink during the Tang Dynasty, gradually travelled west, and is now part of our everyday lives. In China and Japan, the tea ceremony is an act of meditation, a contemplative symbol of spiritual enlightenment. Though a more noisy ritual in the west, tea is also seen as a blessed brew whose benefits extend beyond the conversational and into the cosmetic. Many beauty products employ black and green tea for their antioxidants, and teabags are an excellent home remedy for swollen eyes and bee stings. Some studies have shown that tea can help with high blood pressure, cholesterol and osteoporosis. Presentation is also an important part of tea drinking so take care when packaging this precious commodity. Natural containers are suitable as they reflect the tea's natural origins. Wrap loose teas in vegetable-dyed muslin and place them in a grass container. Cups are also an important part of the tea drinking ritual, so choose beautiful shapes of fine porcelain and wrap up with raffia. Photocopy this label, page 121.

TRAVELLING TEAS

If you're offering a foreign tea, make a paper packet from a
map depicting its origin.
Basic paper packet template, page 122.

PRETTY CONTAINERS

Put bags into pretty boxes that will fall open into a
flower-like container. DIY template, page 122.

NATURAL ORIGINS

Cover a box and lid in glowing yellow and use grass
instead of string for a natural tie.

GOING GREEN

Green tea is a health essential, present it in a tube
sealed with leaves.
Photocopy this label, page 121.

HEALING SPICE

Ask your local watchmaker for these silver containers with transparent lids to hold each spice. Spices may bring sugar and all things nice to mind, but their wonder extends beyond pleasure. Aniseed is excellent for digestion or to freshen your breath, while cinnamon is said to improve circulation, increase the heart rate and treat intestinal disorders. The Ancient Egyptians used cinnamon as an embalming oil and the Chinese regarded it as the Tree of Life. Ginger also appears in tales of ancient cultures, our ginger bread originated when the ancient Greeks wrapped ginger in bread to aid digestion. It is still known for its effective treatment of nausea and motion sickness and is a good cold and flu fighter.

DEVILISH CHILI FAVORITES

Chili con Carne, Harissa, Sweet Chili Sauce, Thai Beef Salad.

WRAPPED BOWL

Fill a bowl with fresh produce, cover with wax paper and finish with a favourite recipe suggestion.

SPICE BOX

Spices are wonderfully sensual, carrying the romance of their exotic origins in their taste and aroma. A tray of spices can evoke thoughts of ancient trading routes where travelling merchants bartered their precious cargo. Used properly, they can transform a simple meal – star anise is a wonderful addition to a tomato-based curry and vanilla seeds in clotted cream make a decadent treat. Ayurveda, the Indian system of health and philosophy, uses spice blends in food and teas to restore and balance the body and mind. Savory spices are thought to calm and relax; sweet aromatic spices, to cool; and pungent spices, to warm. Make a careful selection with your friend, partner, or family member in mind. Use an existing box with a separate lid, cover or spray with non-toxic paint (or use a tin box), and fill with small containers holding your spice selection.

TOMATOES IN A BASKET

Choose the perfect basket for your loved one and fill it with fresh produce. Most of us have forgotten the sublime taste of organically grown, sun-ripened tomatoes – a gift like this could ignite visions of an *al fresco* Italian meal in the Tuscan hills. Suggest a fresh tomato sauce or a picnic of bread, virgin olive oil, and a handful of these delectable morsels.

ROSEHIP HEARTS

Use rosehips to make a decorative wreath. These are sweet table decorations and can be harvested for making rosehip jelly.

HERB BUNDLES

Lovely to look at and sure to penetrate the air with deliciousness.
Tie into a bunch and fasten the ends of the ribbon into a loop for hanging. They can be used fresh or hung to dry, either way they'll add flavor to food and are great for general well-being.

HEALING HERBS

Origanum will help with indigestion.
Lavender will soothe you to sleep
and help cure a headache.
Rosemary is balancing and
invigorates the senses.
Thyme is associated with happiness
and courage.
Mint stimulates a fading appetite.
Mustard seeds should be chewed
when a cold is threatening.

NAME TAGS

Make tags to identify herbs. Cut
a popsicle stick, using a small
saw, so that one end is pointed
and the other flat. Paint with
blackboard paint and attach a
piece of chalk for writing. If you
have the correct tools you can
make these tags using slate.

A BASKET OF EGGS

Eggs are symbols of renewal
and life. Their polished shells
and perfect shape make them a
good basket filler and they're a
kitchen essential.

HARISSA PASTE

A potent product to be used according to tolerance – this is super hot so treat it carefully. Package in a glass jar covered with a black and white print of other Egyptian wonders.
Recipe, page 118.

SUPER SALTS

Make salty blends to spice up the table. For a herb-infused salt, crush 150 g/6 oz of coarse sea salt, mix in 45 ml/3 tbsp of dried herbs. Alternatively, mix 100 g/4 oz of dry roasted sesame seeds with 30 g/1 oz of sea salt. Toast the seeds over a low heat until they begin to turn golden. Dukkah is also a salt supplement, delicious with fresh bread dipped in olive oil or with boiled eggs. Dukkah is best eaten fresh, but leave the sesame and herb salts for a week or so before giving away.
Egyptian Dukkah recipe, page 118.

FLAVORED VINEGARS

These will add an infused edge to food. Use lemon grass vinegar in Vietnamese dishes and stir-fries, tarragon in bearnaise sauce, salad dressings, and chicken or fish marinades, and rose petal over strawberries with a sprinkling of caster sugar.
Recipes, page 118.
Photocopy these labels, page 121.

PICKLED LIMES

Give this lime and chili pickle to someone who adores hot and tasty things. It complements fish, or hot dishes such as curry. Prepare 400 ml/13 fl oz by cutting two limes into slices and spreading them out in a single layer in a colander. Sprinkle 30 ml/2 tbsp of coarse sea salt over them and leave until limp. Remove the pits and arrange the slices in layers in a jar, sprinkling every layer with a pinch or two of chili powder or flakes. Press down lightly and fill the jar with olive oil to cover the top layer. Cover tightly and leave for two or three weeks before using.

SUGARED PINEAPPLES

Great for decorating cakes and ice-cream, or just to snack on. Heat 220 g/9 oz sugar and 250 ml/1 cup water and stir until it dissolves. Bring to the boil and reduce by half. Peel one pineapple, cut into thin slices and pat dry with paper towels. Using a pastry brush, cover both sides with the sugar syrup, and place on a non-stick baking tray. Bake at 100°C/ 212°F/ less than gas 1 until dry and crisp (four to six hours), turning the slices from time to time. Remove from the oven, cool on a wire rack, and store in an airtight container.

PEACH CONSERVE

Old-world jam that captures a piece of summertime and gives the kitchen shelves a homely feel.
Recipe, page 119.

STICKY FIG AND GINGER JAM

Addictive on biscuits. Delicious with cheese and bread.
Recipe, page 119.

A BOWL OF SWEETS

Work with the simple line of a bowl and gorgeous oriental
sweet wrappers for a truly stylish treat. Fill a bowl with
eastern bon-bons, cover in wax paper and tie with
embroidery thread.

FORTUNE-TELLING

Take fortune cookies along to a dinner party, they're bound
to liven things up with their cheerful messages.

NOODLES ON A PLATTER

Add flavor to a simple red platter with a tasty morsel. This eastern-style platter looks great with oriental noodles bound in a Chinese opera invitation. Look for extra elements like these to personalize each offering.

FORTUNE COOKIES IN A BAMBOO BOX

Snack on a couple while preparing the gift and use the extra messages instead of tape to seal.

CHINESE PRINT-LINED BOX
AND MORE NOODLES

A boxed gift is an old-world pleasure. Create a
beautiful, lined box for your gift to nestle in.
Flip-lid template, page 123.

BAMBOO STEAMER AND
MUSLIN-WRAPPED RICE

A gift of organic materials like bamboo and muslin holding an
essential, earthly offering of rice is sublime in its simplicity. A
pretty bead on embroidery thread will pull it all together.

GOOD FOOD FAST

Soothe a frantic soul with this eastern wonder food. Put dry miso ingredients into a bowl, seal with a bamboo lid, wrap in a tea towel, and place a spoon between the folds.

MISO MAGIC

Daily helpings of miso broth have been shown to lower cholesterol, neutralize the negative effects of pollution, and prevent free radical damage. Recipe suggestions, page 119.

UTILITY PICNIC

Kit your favorite sun-seeking couple out with picnic
paraphernalia on their anniversary or when they're
looking particularly work worn. For romantic
lighting, pour wax granules over a wick in a used
cigar tube and, just in case their sight of each other
dulls their faculties, seal these with a gentle
reminder not to leave an open flame unattended.
(Photocopy this label, page 121.) For stylish settings,
tie white enamel plates, elegant wooden forks and
serviettes with printed tape. Order tape with a
choice word – such as "eat" – printed on it. Add a
jar of marinated olives (recipe, page 119),
a baguette, and a bottle of good wine and send
them off into the sunset.

FOR TWO

Let your love nibble on the thought of time together. Attach the promise of a movie for two onto a box of fresh popcorn. A classic romance is in order here, so check your local video store or look out for screenings of *Gone with the Wind, Love Story, Casablanca, Romeo and Juliet, The Way We Were, Breakfast at Tiffany's, From Here to Eternity,* and other fairy-tale flicks. Photocopy this label, page 121.

SWEETS FOR MY SWEET

A tray for your treasure – perfect for nights in or apart.

FORGET-ME-NOT MERINGUES

Tie up a fanciful meringue in forget-me-not tape and place it in a box covered in rice paper interwoven with hearts for a tender, whimsical declaration. Flip-lid box template, page 123.

CHILI VODKA

A drink to share that should track a torrid trail through your body. Prepare this intoxicating potion by pouring vodka into a sexy bottle and adding three red and three green chilies, seal with a red label printed with suggestive ideas (the definition of "hot", for example) and leave for at least two weeks. For thick, syrupy shots, freeze the vodka in an ice covering. Fill a plastic container larger than your vodka bottle – two-liter mineral water bottles cut along the top are perfect. Place petals, flowers or chilies inside, immerse the bottle in it and place in the freezer. When you're ready, remove from the freezer and place briefly in hot water to loosen the outer plastic. You can use the frozen cover as an ice bucket.

an elegant bow

soft velvet ribbon

multi-colored

paper art

indian prayer sheets

pure linen and buttons

funky bubble wrap

experiment

take-away boxes

encase, enclose, enfold

bearing gifts

tied up with string

close with a sparkly clasp

chinese newsprint

earthy raffia

perfect felt

happy wares

WRAP

Tie wraps

SOAP BALLS
Perfectly round gifts can be wrapped in tissue and twisted to close. Cut a square to fit around your gift, bring the ends together and twist.

CELLOPHANE PACKETS FILLED WITH ALMONDS
Tie wraps are the answer to irregularly shaped gifts. Use festive cellophane to make a packet and close with a little whimsical beadwork.
Basic paper packet template, page 122.

SWEET WRAPPER
Wrap small gifts or sweets in paper folded to resemble candy wrapping.
Folding instructions, page 120.

ANTIQUE HANDKERCHIEF AND VELVET RIBBON
Use an antique hanky or embroider a beautiful cotton one if you have more time. A starched hanky will be easier to work with. Close with a soft velvet ribbon.

FESTIVE EASTER EGGS
Bright pipe cleaners are great substitutes for string or ribbon.

BOUND WITH STRING
A double layer of tissue paper bound in string forming different patterns looks festive and can be hung on the Christmas tree.

LEAF WRAP
Folded leaves are a beautiful alternative to paper, use flexible leaves that don't tear easily. Tie with raffia for a natural look.
Folding instructions, page 120.

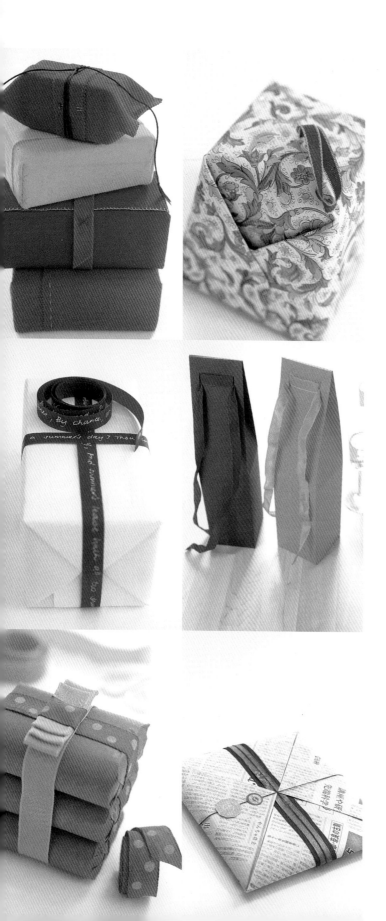

Ribbon wraps

GARLAND WRAP

This is a wonderful way to lead up to a birthday. Place evocative gifts in separate boxes, tie them together with ribbon and give instructions on which present to open on a given day. This also makes a great advent calendar.

FELT AND STITCHING

Touchy-feely felt is perfect for wrapping – it's pliable, doesn't fray, and comes in gorgeous colors. Use basic embroidery stitching to fasten.

FLORENTINE PANETTONE BOX

Use an existing *panettone* box, update the look by sticking decorative paper onto it, and finish with a piece of ribbon.

PRINTED RIBBON

Create your own ribbon by writing messages or poems on paper and cutting it into strips.

FESTIVE WINE BOXES WITH RIBBON DETAILING

The answer to awkward bottles and their give-away shape.
Wine box template, page 123.

INDIVIDUAL WRAPS

Give someone more to open with individually wrapped gifts. Hold them together with an elegant bow.

LAYERED WRAP

Recycle attractive bits and pieces to make your gift a masterpiece. Use a theme, like this eastern-influenced wrap of Chinese newsprint, ribbon, and stamps from a bar of Chinese soap.

Tubes

Remove the label from a tennis ball tube, cover with tracing paper, fill with shredded paper and use as packaging for breakable or fragile gifts.

POSTCARD COVERS
Buy postcards to wrap around tubes before they're filled. Use an existing tube with a diameter equal to that of a rolled postcard. Cut the postcard to the required length, paste it onto the surface and then secure your gift label using a rubber band.

PHOTO TUBE

Make a black and white photocopy of a photograph of
your choice. Scale it to the size you require, use to cover a
tube, and add a personalized message.

PACKING TAPE TIES

Tie a few tubes together with packing tape and present
them as one parcel.

Utility wraps

VIDEO BOX WITH DYMO RIBBON
Instead of discarding promotional video boxes, use them as practical and sturdy packaging for presents. Type your greeting onto Dymo tape and stick it around the gift.

PANETTONE IN A TIN
Recycle those industrial plastic sheets used to protect electronic goods to give an old classic a contemporary look. Tie wrap a cake in spongy plastic and attach a double-folding label onto the end of an embroidery thread tie.

BALLS WRAPPED IN NEWSPAPER
Round goodies are always difficult to wrap, so use pliant tissue paper to cover your gift first. Follow this with a layer of sweet papers or newspaper. Finish with elastic, thin steel wire, or colorful electric wire.

TIN BOX WITH SYMBOLS
International symbols like male/female, knife/fork and camping, to name a few, give a contemporary, fun look. They're available in stencils or stickers and look great against plain backgrounds.

BUBBLE WRAP AND STICKERS
Functional and funky bubble wrap no longer needs covering or hiding away. Carry the postage theme through with 'fragile' stickers.

FILM CANISTERS IN PLASTIC NETTING
Plastic film canisters are useful for holding small gifts. Always keep an eye out for elements to complement the theme of the wrapping you choose – a slide mount with a little photo of the person you are giving the present to slipped into it as a tag, for example.

FOIL WRAP AND UTILITY FASTENINGS

Everyday cooking materials like foil and wax paper double well as gift wrap. Spray mount foil onto paper before wrapping so the foil won't crease. Keep things simple by using utility finishes like paper clips, bull clips, string, or rubber bands.

BOTTLE WRAPPED IN CUT-OUT PLASTIC

Recycle plastic used for transporting breakables to create a retro gift look. Simply cut to size and secure with double-sided tape.

MIXED MEDIUMS

Wrap a parcel in a luxurious fabric, like silk, and close with a bandage clip.

FOIL CONTAINERS

Pack a selection of presents into foil containers, stamp the lids with generic messages like "not transferable," and tie up with electric wire, steel wire, or string.

INNER FOIL

Another answer to wrapping round shapes is to recycle the inside of a potato chip bag. Turn the bag inside out, wash well with soap and warm water, and secure with double-sided tape.

UTILITY TAG

Use an engraved metal dog tag on a bath chain to create a slick, contemporary label.

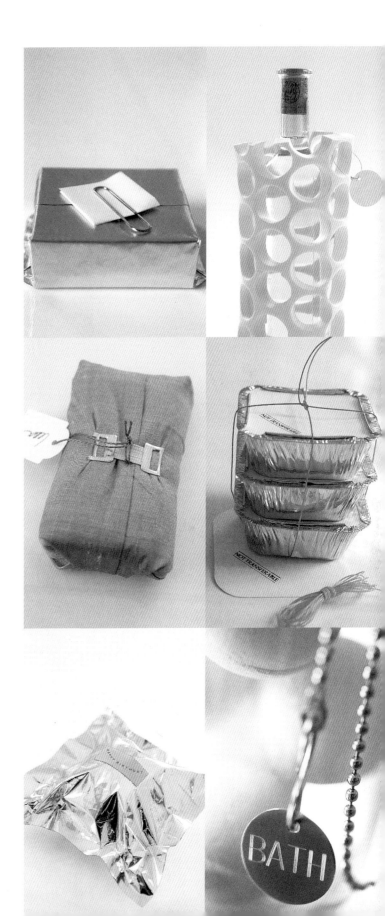

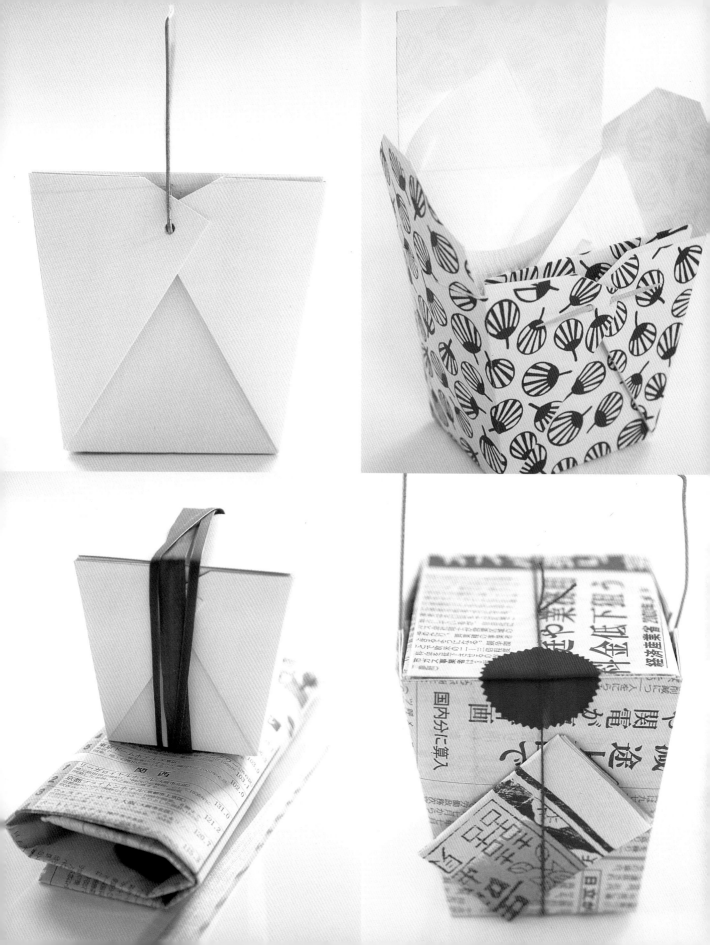

Chinese take-away boxes

BASIC CHINESE TAKE-AWAY BOX
Chinese take-away boxes have been immortalized in American movies, but their simple shape makes a wonderful gift container too. Use the template on page 122 to put the box together – be sure to use card or paper of at least 280 g.

FAN PAPER
Stick decorative oriental paper onto 280 g card and use it to make a take-away box. Nestle a gift in tissue, rice paper, or any lightweight paper.

GRASS TIES
Omit the handle and tie with grass or other natural materials reflecting the eastern spirit.

MATERIAL NEEDS
Experiment with different materials to change the appearance of your packaging. Stick Chinese newsprint onto 280 g card and use this to make up your box or fold raffia over the sides and secure with double-sided tape.

SMALL, MEDIUM, OR LARGE
Size the box according to your needs.
A multi-colored array of 5 cm/2 in high, 120 g card boxes secured with a single cross-stitch and double-sided tape are great for a variety of smaller gifts.

Separate-lid boxes

LIFT THE LID

Boxes do not have to be closed. Stand a box in its lid and place delectable edibles or pampering bath products wrapped in cellophane inside. Finish with ribbon and a gift card.

ZEN BOX

Give a manila box a new look. Cut a strip of white paper to the required length, secure it onto the inside of the lid with double-sided tape and paste a small Japanese print on top.

PHOTO BOX

Boxes with separate lids are difficult to make so recycle existing boxes and cover them to achieve the look you desire. For an upmarket feel, cover the base in white paper and the lid with textured black paper. To use a box for storage, paste an appropriate picture on the lid – an old photo for a box filled with special family pictures, for example.

LINEN-COVERED BOX WITH BUTTONS

Turn a simple box into something special and tactile by covering it in pure linen. Finish with mother-of-pearl buttons. Sew thread onto each button ending with a knot on the back and stick them down using non-toxic glue or a glue gun.

Flip-lid boxes

FOREIGN COVERS

Most of us become avid gatherers when we travel abroad, collecting odds and ends to recall a scrumptious meal, a beautiful painting, a haunting moment. Share your memories by using that Indian prayer sheet, subway map, or wine-stained paper place-mat with your order scrawled across it as wrapping. Write your message on the back of a small flag: use cocktail flags or make a color photocopy from an atlas, and attach with a toothpick. A piece of plastic stuck just under the lid will make it easier to attach.

THE BASICS

Basic flip-lid template, page 123.

NEAT HANDLES

Thread wire through a piece of plastic tube to make a handle. Shape the ends, tie your package up with string and hook the ends of the handle onto it.

A STAMP TO CLOSE

Stamps have been enjoyed by collectors for centuries. They are intriguing for the history they portray, telling of monarchies, people, art, and culture in their intricate design. Collect them on your travels, wander down to your local Post Office and flip through their specialist selection, or find a second-hand store with a collection of old postcards and steam off their wonderful stamps. Place a favorite over the opening of a colorful box.

PAPER PACKAGES TIED UP WITH STRING

Cover a box in white paper or paper with a slight texture and secure with double-sided tape. Tie ordinary kitchen string around the parcel, ending with a loop at the top. Melt sealing wax onto a corner and stamp with a seal.

PATTERNED WRAPPING

Design your wrapping to suit the recipient's passion. Use elements from their trade to decorate their gift – pins and a dress pattern for a clothing designer, or measuring tape and draughtsman's sketches for an architect.

INSIDE AND OUT

Experiment with different materials and paper to contrast the inside and outside of a box. Use a stencil or computer to make a personalized message for the inside of the lid.

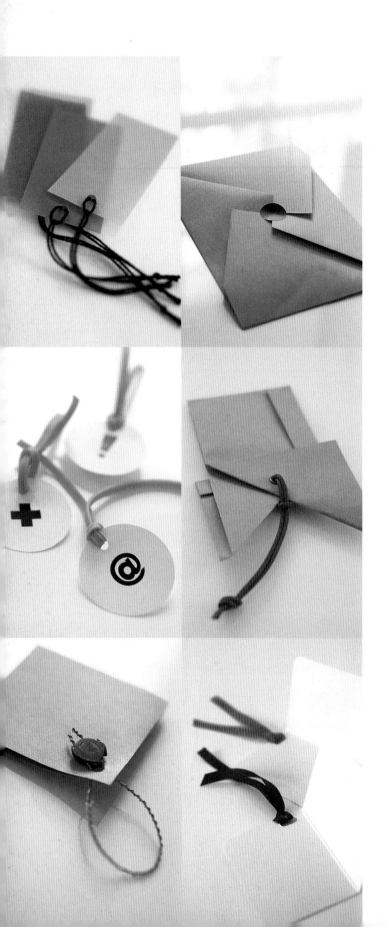

Cards and envelopes

STAMPED GREETINGS
Collect a few stamps of general messages like thank you and Merry Christmas – stationers often have a selection, or have them tailor-made. Use different inks to stamp messages onto plain cards.

FLOATY TAGS
Use tracing paper to make light, floaty tags.

FOLDED ENVELOPES
Fold specially selected paper into an envelope and seal with a plain sticker. This is a great way to present a gift voucher or a small, flat gift.

DIGITAL SYMBOLS
Perfect for the computer fan or the office addict. Enlarge computer-generated symbols on a photocopier, cut into circles, and tie with elastic.
Photocopy these symbols, page 121.

ORIGAMI ENVELOPE
Origami turns paper into art. Impress with this envelope to be used as wrapping or a tag.
Folding instructions, page 120.

WIRE TAGS
Bottles and jars often have beautiful ties around them. Re-use these for a dressy gift tag.

BRIGHT FINISHES
Add a little ribbon glamour to a plain white tag.

Baie Dankie

Recipes

ALMOND CHOCOLATE DATES
Makes about 18

100 g/4 oz whole almonds
250 g/10 oz pitted dates
1 tub marzipan
250 g/10 oz dark chocolate
100 g/4 oz white chocolate

Place one almond in the cavity of each date and add a little marzipan. Melt the dark chocolate in a double boiler. With a toothpick, gently roll the stuffed date in the chocolate and place aside to set. Once set, melt the white chocolate and drizzle or pipe over the dates. Place in mini paper cases. Do not refrigerate.

BASIC BISCUIT MIX

85 g/3$^{1}/_{2}$ oz icing sugar, sifted
30 ml/2 tbsp caster sugar
100 g/4 oz butter, diced
1 egg
2$^{1}/_{2}$ ml/$^{1}/_{2}$ tsp vanilla essence
280 g/11 oz plain flour, sifted

Put the icing and caster sugar into the bowl of a food processor and pulse a few times to mix. Add the butter and process until the mixture resembles fine bread crumbs. Lightly mix the egg and vanilla essence, pour onto the mixture while the machine is running, and add the flour. When the mixture comes together, transfer to a lightly floured surface and work quickly until smooth. Shape the dough into a flat slab and wrap in plastic wrap. Chill until firm. (The dough will keep in the refrigerator for up to a week. To freeze, wrap in a layer of kitchen foil. Defrost in the refrigerator before using.) Cut into shapes and bake in a preheated oven at 200°C/400°F/ gas mark 6 for 8 to 10 minutes or until golden. Leave on racks to cool.

To make conventionally: mix the icing sugar, caster sugar, and butter until creamy. Add the egg and vanilla essence, then the flour and knead to a firm dough.

LAVENDER HEARTS
Makes 25 biscuits

125 g/5 oz butter, at room temperature
60 g/2 oz caster sugar
200 g/8 oz plain flour
30 ml/2 tbsp dried lavender flowers

Cream the butter and caster sugar together until light and fluffy. Add flour and lavender and knead until smooth. Roll dough to 3 mm thickness on a floured surface. Cut into heart shapes and place on a lightly greased baking tray. Bake in a preheated oven at 200°C/400°F/gas mark 6 for 8 to 10 minutes, or until firm. Transfer to wire racks. (The dough can also be made in a food processor.)

MILK AND HONEY BREAD
Makes one loaf

450 g/1 lb 2 oz all-purpose flour
10 g/¹⁄₃ oz instant yeast
5 ml/1 tsp salt
275 ml/9 fl oz milk, heated to lukewarm
15 ml/1 tbsp sugar
30 ml/2 tbsp honey

Put the flour, yeast, and salt into a large mixing bowl. Stir the sugar and honey into the warm milk and add to the flour, mixing until the flour is absorbed. Knead the dough until smooth, for about five minutes. (If it seems too dry, add a little more warm milk.) Shape the dough into a ball, place in a lightly oiled bowl, and cover with plastic wrap. Leave to rise in a warm place until
doubled in volume, for about an hour. Turn the dough out onto a floured surface, punch down, and shape it into an oval loaf. Place in a well greased 18 by 12 cm/ 7¹⁄₄ by 4³⁄₄ in bread tin. Cover and, again, allow to rise in a warm place until doubled in size. Meanwhile, pre-heat the oven to 200°C/400°F/ gas mark 6. Brush the loaf with a little milk, bake for 30 to 35 minutes or until the loaf sounds hollow when tapped on the base.

PISTACHIO NUT COOKIES
Makes about 40

Roll basic biscuit dough (see opposite) out on a floured surface to 3 mm thickness. Cut out 5 cm/2 in rounds. Place the cookies on a baking tray lined with non-stick baking paper, brush with egg glaze, and press a pista-chio nut into the center. If the pistachios are salted, rub in a tea towel to remove salt and skins. Bake in a pre-heated oven at 200°C/400°F/gas mark 6 for 8 to 10 minutes or until golden. Leave on racks to cool.

CHOCOLATE AND ALMOND BISCOTTI
Makes about 36 biscuits

250 g/10 oz plain flour
250 g/10 oz caster sugar
5 ml/1 tsp baking powder
2 eggs, lightly beaten
2.5 ml/¹⁄₂ tsp vanilla essence
50 g/2 oz chocolate chips or plain chocolate, chopped

100 g/4 oz almonds, toasted and coarsely chopped

Sift the flour, caster sugar, and baking powder into a mixing bowl and make a well in the center. Mix the beaten egg with the vanilla essence and pour into the well, slowly working the flour into a dough. Stir in the almonds and chocolate. Divide the dough in two, roll out into flat log shapes of about 4 cm/1¹⁄₂ in wide and place on a baking sheet lined with non-stick baking paper. Leave enough room between the logs for the mixture to spread. Bake in a preheated oven at 180°C/ 350°F/gas mark 4 for 25 to 30 minutes or until golden brown. Remove from the oven and reduce the oven temperature to 150°C/300°F/gas mark 2. Slice the logs at an angle into 1 cm/¹⁄₂ in pieces. Return them to the oven for another 30 minutes or until dry. Cool on a wire rack and store in an airtight container.

CITRUS COOLER

500 ml/1 pt water
100 g/4 oz granulated sugar
rind of 1 orange, in large pieces
rind of 1 lemon, in large pieces
1 vanilla pod, split lengthwise
4 sprigs fresh mint
500 m/2 cups orange juice, freshly squeezed
200 ml/7fl oz lemon juice, freshly squeezed
300 ml/10 fl oz grapefruit juice, freshly squeezed
vodka (optional)

Combine the water, sugar, orange and lemon rind, vanilla pod, and mint sprigs in a medium saucepan. Stir to dissolve sugar and bring to the boil. Remove from heat and cool. Strain. (This syrup can be stored in the refrigerator until ready to use.) Mix the syrup with the citrus juices, pour into a suitable container and freeze until crystals begin to form. Break down crystals with a fork and pour into chilled glasses. Garnish with mint sprigs and lemon slices. Alternatively, chill mixture and serve over crushed ice topped with a splash of vodka.

OATMEAL BISCUITS
Makes 25 biscuits

100 g/4 oz oatmeal
100 g/4 oz wholewheat flour
2.5 ml/1/2 tsp bicarbonate of soda
2.5 ml/1/2 tsp salt
50 g/2 oz cold butter, cut into cubes
50 g/2 oz lard, cut into cubes
30 g/1 oz soft brown sugar
15-30 ml/1-2 tbsp milk

Lightly mix the dry ingredients. Rub in the butter and lard. (If you don't want to use lard, use 100 g/4 oz butter instead). Add the sugar and mix to a firm dough with a little milk.

To make in a food processor: blend all the ingredients, except the milk, to resemble fine breadcrumbs. Add just enough milk to make a firm dough. Roll out onto a floured surface to a 4 mm thickness. Cut into 5 cm/2 in circles and bake on a lightly buttered baking tray in a preheated oven at 180°C/350°F/gas mark 4 for 15 minutes.

MULLED WINE
Makes six glasses

1 bottle dry red wine
30 ml/2 tbsp brown sugar
For spice bag:
4 whole cloves
1 cinnamon stick
6 cardamom seeds, crushed
For garnish:
strips of orange rind

Put the wine, sugar, and spice bag into a saucepan. Very slowly bring it just to boiling point, stirring to dissolve the sugar. Remove from the heat, cover with a lid and allow flavors to infuse for 10 minutes. Remove spice bag. Place strips of orange rind in glasses and top with warm wine.

FLORENTINES
Makes 24

50 g/2 oz caster sugar
40 g/1 1/2 oz butter
30 ml/2 tbsp cream
15 ml/1 tbsp flour
50 g/2 oz flaked almonds
50 g/2 oz glacé cherries (red and green) and mixed candied peel, chopped
50 g/2 oz white chocolate, melted

Put all the ingredients (except the white chocolate) into a saucepan and stir over low heat until blended. Drop teaspoonfuls of the mixture well apart onto two baking trays lined with non-stick baking paper and flatten with a wet fork. Bake in a preheated oven at 180°C/350°F/gas mark 4 for 10 minutes, or until the edges are golden brown. To make perfect circles, place a cookie cutter over each florentine and lightly press with a fork. Leave on the baking sheet until firm, then cool on a wire rack. Spread melted chocolate over the smooth side of each biscuit (give them a second coat if needed). Use a fork to make wavy lines. Leave until the chocolate cools and hardens.

To melt chocolate: break chocolate into a small mixing bowl and place over a saucepan of hot water. Leave for about five minutes, then stir until smooth.

LEBKUCHEN
Makes 55-60

115 g/4½ oz butter
115 g/4½ oz soft brown sugar
90 g/3½ oz treacle or molasses
1 egg
280 g/12 oz plain flour
5 ml/1 tsp baking powder
10 ml/2 tsp ground ginger
5 ml/1 tsp ground cinnamon
Royal icing:
170 g/7 oz icing sugar, sifted
1 egg white

Cream the butter and sugar. Add the treacle or molasses and egg, and mix until smooth. Sift the dry ingredients together. Stir into the butter and sugar, and mix to form a stiff dough. Chill until firm. Roll out to 3 mm thickness and cut into moon shapes. Place on a baking sheet lined with non-stick baking paper and bake in a preheated oven at 180°C/350°F/gas mark 4 for 10 minutes. Leave to cool. Mix icing sugar and egg white to a smooth consistency and, holding the biscuit carefully, dip it into the icing to cover the top. Leave on a wire rack to let the icing set and dry.

STEAMED LEMON SPONGE PUDDING
Serves six

100 g/4 oz butter
100 g/4 oz caster sugar
2 eggs, beaten
grated rind of 2 lemons
140 g/6 oz self-raising flour
5 ml/1 tsp baking powder
90 ml/3 fl oz lemon juice
45 ml/3 tbsp lemon marmalade

Cream the butter and sugar until light and fluffy. Gradually beat in the eggs, then add the lemon rind. Sieve the flour and baking powder, and fold into the creamed mixture using the lemon juice to mix it to a soft dropping consistency. Butter a 2 liter/1 qt bowl. Warm the marmalade a little, spread in the base of the bowl, and spoon over the mixture. Cover the bowl with buttered baking paper, making a generous fold across the top and tie down with string. Place bowl in a large saucepan, add hot water to come halfway up the bowl and steam for one-and-a-half hours, checking the water level from time to time. Remove the pudding from the mold and place on a serving plate. Serve with lemon curd or with a 'custard' made by mixing equal parts hot cream and lemon curd.

To make in the microwave: cover the bowl with plastic wrap. Microwave at full power for 6 minutes. Remove, pierce a few holes in the plastic wrap and cover the top of bowl with a dinner plate. Leave for 10 minutes.

LEMON CURD
Makes 250 ml/1 cup

125 g/5 oz unsalted butter, cubed
100 g/4 oz caster sugar
60 ml/2 tbsp lemon juice
grated zest of 1 lemon
3 eggs, beaten and strained

Melt the butter and add sugar, lemon juice, and zest. Stir to dissolve the sugar and remove from the heat. Whisk a little of the hot mixture into the eggs and pour them into the saucepan, beating well with a wooden spoon. Return to a medium heat and stir until thick – do not allow to boil. Cool and pour into a sterilized jar. This will keep in the fridge for up to two weeks.

To make in the microwave: place butter, sugar, juice and zest in a glass bowl and cover with plastic wrap. Microwave at full power for 4 minutes. Remove from the microwave and stir well. Whisk a little of the hot mixture into the eggs and pour them into the lemon mixture while whisking. Cook, uncovered, at full power for 2 minutes. Whisk until smooth, return to the microwave and cook for another minute on the same power. (At this stage it might curdle.) Remove from the microwave and immediately pour into the container of a food processor. Process until smooth. Cool and pour into a sterilized jar.

HARISSA PASTE
Makes one small jar

25 large dried red chilies, seeds removed
3 cloves garlic, chopped
5 ml/1 tbsp mustard seeds
5 ml/1 tsp sea salt
125 ml/4 fl oz olive oil, plus 30 ml/2 tbsp extra

This is best made using a small hand blender. Failing that, pound the ingredients using a pestle and mortar. Place the chilies in a bowl and cover them with hot water. Leave to soak for an hour, drain and dry with paper towels. Use kitchen scissors to cut the chilies into small pieces. Blend or pound the chilies, garlic, mustard seeds, and salt until quite fine. Add the olive oil, a little at a time, to make a thin paste. Spoon it into a sterilized jar and pour the extra olive oil on top. Seal and store in the refrigerator for up to 12 months.

EGYPTIAN DUKKAH

100 g/4 oz hazelnuts
100 g/4 oz sesame seeds
50 g/2 oz cumin seeds
30 ml/2 tbsp ground coriander
5 ml/1 tsp ground cinnamon
5 ml/1 tsp coarsely ground sea salt
2.5 ml/1/2 tsp crushed black peppercorns

Roast hazelnuts in a preheated oven at 180°C/350°F/ gas mark 4 for 10 minutes, then rub in a clean teatowel to remove the skins. Dry roast the sesame seeds in a pan over gentle heat until they change color. Roast the cumin seeds in the same way. Put all the ingredients in a blender or processor and process until fine. Store in jars with tightly fitting lids in a cool, dark place.

LEMONGRASS-FLAVORED RICE VINEGAR
Makes 300 ml/11 fl oz

300 ml/11 fl oz rice vinegar
3–4 stalks of lemongrass
Trim lemongrass to fit the bottle. Pound the stalks to release the flavor. Put the lemongrass into the bottle and fill with rice vinegar. Leave to one week to infuse,

then store in the refrigerator.

TARRAGON VINEGAR
Makes 300 ml/11 fl oz

handful of fresh tarragon leaves
300 m/11 fl oz white wine vinegar
sprigs of fresh tarragon

Bruise the tarragon leaves by rubbing them with your fingers, add to the vinegar, and warm over low heat. Pour into a suitable container, cover, and leave to infuse for two weeks. Strain. Put the fresh tarragon sprigs into a sterilized bottle and fill with the strained vinegar. Store in a cool, dark place.

ROSE PETAL VINEGAR
Makes 300 ml/11 fl oz
(Do not use roses that were sprayed with pesticides)

375 ml/13 fl oz fragrant red rose petals
300 ml/11 fl oz white wine vinegar

Put the rose petals into a clean wide-necked glass bottle. Heat the vinegar over moderate heat until warm to the touch and pour over the rose petals. Push the petals down to immerse them in the vinegar. Allow the vinegar to cool to room temperature and seal the bottle. Leave the vinegar in a cool, dark place until it has turned bright red – this will take about one week. Strain to remove the petals. Put a few fresh petals in a clean sterilized bottle (use chopsticks to push them down) and fill with the strained vinegar. Seal and label. The vinegar will keep at room temperature for up to six months.

PEACH CONSERVE
Makes 1 1/2 kg/3 lb

500 g/1 lb sun-dried peaches
1 litre/2 pt water
1 kg/2.2 lb granulated sugar
30 ml/2 tbsp brandy
100 g/4 oz flaked almonds (optional)

Rinse and soak peaches in cold water overnight. Drain.
Pour the water and sugar into a large saucepan and
bring slowly to a boil while stirring to dissolve sugar.
Add peaches and simmer for an hour or until setting
point is reached and peaches are soft but not cooked
to a pulp. Remove from heat and stir in brandy and
almonds (if using) and leave to cool. Ladle into
sterilized jars and seal.

STICKY FIG AND GINGER JAM

500 g/1 lb ripe figs
500 g/1 lb green figs
800 g/1 lb 12 oz sugar
2 pieces of dry ginger
juice of 1 lemon

Cover figs with hot water and leave for a minute or
two. Drain. Remove stems, cut into quarters, place in a
large pan and cover with sugar. Heat over low heat
until sugar has dissolved, shaking the pan from time to
time to distribute the sugar. Add ginger and lemon
juice. Increase the heat and bring to the boil, stirring
frequently. When the fruit is soft and the syrup thick,
remove from heat. Cool and pour into sterilized jars
and cover tightly.

MISO SOUP
One serving

Prepare the soup according to the packet instructions,
then add the following:

tofu, cut into small cubes
dried wakame seaweed, cut into pieces
small piece of poached salmon
prepared Japanese noodles
spring onions, finely sliced

MARINATED OLIVES
Makes about 400 ml/14 fl oz

250 g/10 oz drained black olives
1 lime
3 sprigs of fresh thyme
2 garlic cloves, peeled and halved lengthwise
olive oil

Make two or three slits in each olive. Cut the limes
into thin slices and halve each slice. Layer the olives
and lime slices in a wide-necked sterilized jar, and
push the thyme sprigs and garlic halves down the
sides. Cover the olives with the olive oil, seal and
marinate for one to two weeks in the refrigerator.
Serve at room temperature.

Paper projects

BASIC KIT
Steel ruler
Scissors
Craft knife
Tracing wheel
Carbon paper
Double-sided tape
Spray mount
Glue gun
Cutting mat
Hole Puncher
Small pliers

SWEET WRAPPER

Light or medium-weight paper

Photocopy the template to enlarge or reduce to your required size. Make a pattern by tracing image onto graph or tracing paper. Cut it out, place on wrong side of the paper and draw around the pattern on the paper indicating the folding line. Using a craft knife and steel ruler, cut out the marked rectangular pieces of paper. Place paper wrong side up and position the sweet or gift just above the folding line. Fold bottom edge up, fold up the bottom corners at an angle so that the corners slightly overlap the edge of the first fold. Fold to overlap the side edges and twist top end to finish.

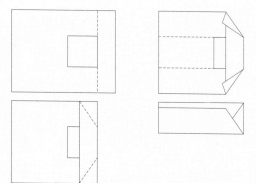

TRIANGLE LEAF WRAP

Large flexible leaves
Raffia or sisal cord to tie

Photocopy the template to enlarge or reduce to your required size. Cut or tear long strips of leaves using the template as a guide. Wrap gift in tracing paper to form a triangular shape. Place on bottom edge of leaf strip and start rolling upward by folding the bottom edge to line up with the left edge. Continue this rolling motion along the entire strip and secure with raffia or string.

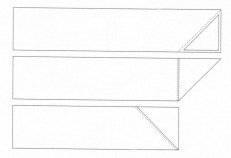

ORIGAMI ENVELOPE WRAP

Medium-weight paper – standard letter size

Fold paper in half lengthwise, wrong sides facing. Make a double fold of 1 1/2 cm/**5/8** in lengthwise on the open edge. Fold in half widthwise, leaving the double fold to show on the outside of the envelope. Fold the opposite top corners down to form a right angle with the envelope. Secure with an eyelet and string or cord.

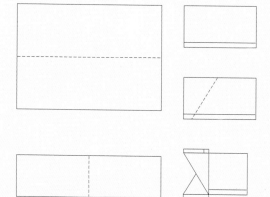

Labels

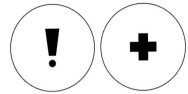

! + @    ☆

Thé

ADMISSION

MOVIE TICKET FOR 2

RIGHT OF ADMISSION RESERVED

S.W.E.E.T DREAMS
○

CAUTION, THIS DRINK IS HOT

FRESH FEET Peppermint, Teatree, Sandalwood, Menthol for a tingling antiseptic treat for your feet.

Green Tea

DON'T LEAVE AN OPEN FLAME UNATTENDED

CHILL OUT

VANILLA INFUSED BRANDY

ORANGE INFUSED BRANDY

CINNAMON INFUSED BRANDY

HOT
CHOCOLATE
CREAM

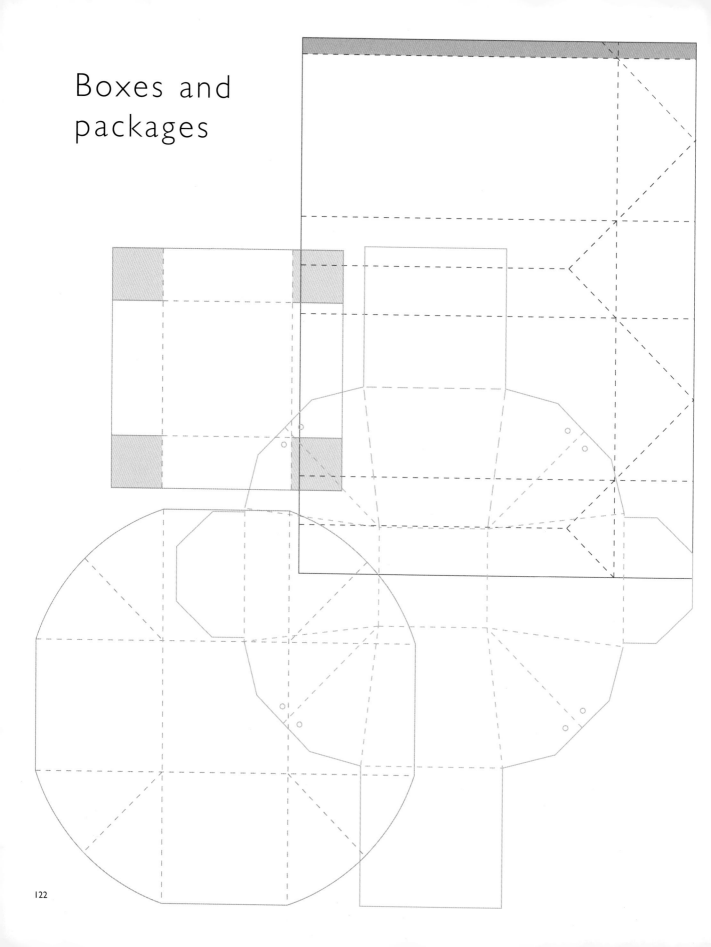

Boxes and
packages

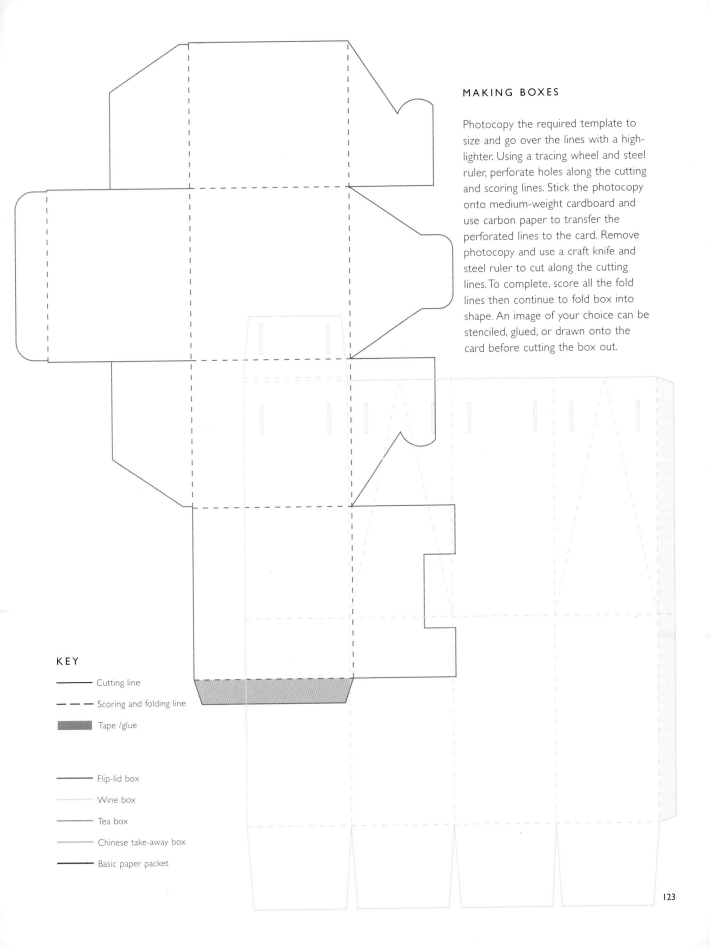

MAKING BOXES

Photocopy the required template to size and go over the lines with a highlighter. Using a tracing wheel and steel ruler, perforate holes along the cutting and scoring lines. Stick the photocopy onto medium-weight cardboard and use carbon paper to transfer the perforated lines to the card. Remove photocopy and use a craft knife and steel ruler to cut along the cutting lines. To complete, score all the fold lines then continue to fold box into shape. An image of your choice can be stenciled, glued, or drawn onto the card before cutting the box out.

KEY

———— Cutting line

— — — Scoring and folding line

▨ Tape /glue

——— Flip-lid box

——— Wine box

——— Tea box

——— Chinese take-away box

——— Basic paper packet

Sewing projects

BASIC SEWING KIT

Good quality plain edge scissors
Embroidery scissors
Pinking shears
Metal tape measure and small plastic ruler
Steel dressmaking pins
Stitch ripper
Variety of needles for different weights of fabric
Steam iron
Blunt knitting needle for pushing out corners
Sewing machine with plain and zipper foot

BEADED COASTERS

Main fabric
Polyester thread
Matching beads

Cut two 12 cm/4³/₄ in squares from the main fabric. Draw your design freehand on the right side of one of the squares with a soft drawing pencil or tailor's chalk. Mark the design's pattern with dressmaker's pins to represent each bead. Stitch one bead at a time, replacing each pin in turn. Use strong polyester thread the same color as the bead and a long thin needle. Make a large knot in a double thread and pass the needle through the fabric from the back. Thread the bead on and pass the needle through the fabric to the wrong side, finishing off with a few tiny stitches hidden behind the bead. Place beaded and other fabric square right sides facing and sew all sides, leaving a gap on one side. Press the seam allowances along the open edge to the wrong side, clip the corners and turn through, pushing corners out carefully with a blunt knitting needle. Close opening with slip-stitch.

FRENCH LINEN NAPKINS

Linen
Matching thread

Cut 55 cm/22 in squares from the linen. With the fabric right side up, fold over a 1 cm/¹/₂ in return on all sides and press. Leaving the return in place, fold over a 4 cm/1¹/₂ in seam on all sides and press. Unfold the seam and fold in the corners so the diagonal fold aligns with the straight fold lines in the seam. Trim off excess fabric across the corner leaving just less than 1 cm/¹/₂ in seam allowance. Turn in one seam along the seam line, crease to form a neat corner, press and tack. Continue to turn in seams on all sides, forming neat corners; press and tack. Top-stitch hem in place close to the edge with matching thread. Finish the corners with slip-stitch. Finished width 45 cm/18 in.

CUTLERY HOLDER

Main fabric
Lining
Cotton tape

Cut 84 cm by 53 cm/ 33¹/₂ x 21 in rectangles from the main fabric and lining, and cut a 80 cm/32 in length of cotton tape. Place the main fabric and lining right sides together and stitch all sides, leaving a gap on one short side. Press the seam allowances along the open edge to the wrong side, trim the seams, clip the corners and turn right side out, pushing corners out carefully with closed scissors. Press well and close the opening by hand or machine stitch. Top-stitch along the edge of one of the long sides, fold over 14 cm/5¹/₂ in to the lining side and pin and tack side seams to make a pocket. Pin and tack 5 cm/2 in inserts along the pocket to hold the cutlery. Stitch in inserts on the pocket, oversewing at the top to reinforce pocket edge. Insert the tape in the left pocket seam (50 cm/ 20 in from the left end of the tape) and about 2 cm/1 in from the top edge of the pocket. Top stitch along the edge of two short sides and one long side, but not the bottom edge of the pocket (the folded edge). Reinforce pocket seams with a second top-stitch. Insert cutlery, fold over top edge of cutlery holder to meet top of pocket, roll up from right to left, and tie up tape.

SEWING KIT

Felt
Silk lining
Cotton tape

Cut 32 cm by 17 cm/ 13 x 7 in rectangles from felt and
lining. Cut two 10 cm by 8 cm/ 4 x 3 in
rectangles of felt with pinking shears to form a"booklet"
to hold pins. Cut a 20 cm/8 in length of cotton tape to
hold sewing materials/equipment. Pin the felt "booklet"
and the tape onto the right side of the lining and sew.
Stitch in inserts on the tape to hold thimbles and other
bits and pieces. Place the lining and felt right sides
together, insert a piece of narrow ribbon or string to
form a button loop on the short side, and sew two long
sides and one short side with a 1 cm/^{1}/$_2$ in seam
allowance. Turn through and press. Oversew the final
edge. Fold over 5^{1}/$_2$ cm/2^{1}/$_4$ in to the lining side and pin
the side seams to make a pocket. Tack felt and lining
together along the edge of all sides and top stitch,
working from the felt side, to secure pockets. Fold the
sewing kit to close and attach a button.

WHITE SCENTED HEART

Main fabric
Narrow ribbon, string, cord or tape for hanging loop

Cut two 15 cm/6 in squares of the main fabric. Make a
reusable template by tracing/transferring the heart
diagram onto graph or tracing paper. Place the two
squares of fabric right sides facing and cut out the
heart pattern. Insert a piece of narrow ribbon, string or
cord to form a hanging loop in the dip of the heart
and stitch all around leaving a 4 cm/1 ^{1}/$_2$ in opening on
one side. Press the seam allowances along the open
edge to the wrong side, snip the seams on the rounded
edges, and clip the corner, turn through, pushing corner
out carefully with a blunt knitting needle. Stuff with a
mixture of dried petals and polyester fiber filler or
cotton wool. Sprinkle stuffing with a few drops of your
chosen essential oil. Close opening with slip-stitch.
Tip: a great recipe for stuffing is to mix a fiber filler
with a pot-pourri of four tablespoons of rose petals
sprinkled with four drops of Moroccan rose oil.
Sleep-inducing fragrances include: lavender, camomile,
sage, sandalwood, ylang ylang, neroli, and frankincense.

Credits

cover model Amanda James from The Model Company; cardigan Savanna; skirt Hilton Weiner

page 1 herb bundle on sandstone tiles from Just Tiles

page 2 ribbons VV Rouleaux

page 4 right: stamp Le Papier

page 8 model Anniken from Ice Model Management; sweater Hilton Weiner; hot water bottle Spirit

page 10 top and bottom left: beads for coasters Craft Distributers, fabric for coasters, California from Tessa Sonik's Statement range; pouch in Metallic Organza Gold also Tessa Sonik Fabric Collection; tablecloth in Terracotta from the Incense range by Monkwell available at Home Fabrics; glasses Moroccan Warehouse; bottom middle: Beads and leather thongs for bead box Craft Distributers; necklace Daisey Box; top right: bag in Gem Garnet from the Nono Precious Collection available at Home Fabrics; incense LIM; model Amanda James from The Model Company

page 12 cupwarmers in Fiesta Afrique from Orion on sandstone tiles from Just Tiles

page 13 top: hotwater bottle cover in Fiesta Afrique from Orion; fleece throw LIM; bottom: top and jacket Naartjie, trousers Hilton Weiner; fuchsia grosgrain ribbon Paperchase

page 14 top left: cutlery holder in Brandon Blue from Boulders Collection from St Leger & Viney; lining in Base Cloth White Biggie Best, cutlery Spirit, table Weylandts; top right: table runners in Heavy Natural Linen Flax from the Studio Collection at Mavromac; velvet ribbon Castellano Beltrame; glasses Moroccan Warehouse; table, cushions and chairs Weylandts; bottom left: place mats in Alpaca Seaweed and

Greystone from Tessa Sonik; napkins in Fine Christal Linen by OJ van Maehle from Mavromac; bowls by Prêt-à-pot available at Weylandts; side plates LIM; cutlery Spirit; table and chairs Weylandts; bottom right: napkins in Fine Christal Linen by OJ Van Maehle available at Mavromac

page 16-17 table, chairs, console table, glass jug and tablecloth in Voile White all Biggie Best; table runners in Troyer White Linen St Leger & Viney; crockery Loft Living; crystal glasses Fosters; candle glasses Loads of Linen and Living; mirror Block and Chisel; Christmas stockings in Harrigan White from White Mischief Collection at St Leger & Viney; twig Christmas tree sprayed with Plascon Lac-R-Spray Matt White; walls in White Double Velvet and floors in White Velvaglo non-drip Enamel, both Plascon; handbag Daizey Box; model Anniken from Ice Model Management; blouse Salomé Gunter, skirt Juanita Pacheco, Nicola Lotz in tutu from Peggity's; beads (tiara) from Craft Distributers

page 18 star packets in Stardream Opal and Silver from Papersmith & Son; beads from Craft Distributers

page 21 top left: beads for pin cushion Craft Distributers; top right: needlecase in Elemento by Ulf Moritz from Sahco Hesslein available at Home Fabrics, lined in Elitis Taffeta Etat de Grâce available at St Leger & Viney on wooden laminated flooring, Albert Carpets; bottom right: shoebag Spirit; shoes Nina Roche

page 22 top right: notebooks covered in Saville Row from Fabric Library; bottom left: guineafowl feathers Fabulous Flowers; jacket and trousers Polo; bottom right: felt cushions in Elepunto and Elecaro by Ulf Moritz from Sahco Hesslein available at Home Fabrics; ribbon Paperchase; sandstone tiles from Just Tiles

page 24-25 shot on location at Loft

Living, 122 Kloof Street, Gardens 8001, Cape Town; top left: album in Silky Sensuede Fuchsia and Tangerine available at St Leger & Viney; ribbon Paperchase; covered by Handcrafted Photo Albums; top right: Mia Krüger on mouse pad; iMac from Access International, pen and desk Loft Living; bottom left: notebook The Conran Shop; tablecloth in Antique Courtesanne available at Home Fabrics; bottom middle: frames in Courtisane Antique, Wine and Plum available at Home Fabrics. Model Terry from Ice Model Management; bottom right: filofax in Canoletto from Rubelli available at Mavromac; tablecloth in Rust from the Incense range by Monkwell available at Home Fabrics; glasses John-Henry Fox

page 27 left: Thinus Kruger with hand puppets from Ikea, glycerine paper packets Bright House; wooden laminated flooring, Albert Carpets

page 28 left: boats on sandstone tiles from Just Tiles

page 29 left: Thinus Kruger in orange bandanna, Daisey Box

page 30 model Amanda James from The Model Company

page 32 envelopes in Sunset and Sweet Pea from the Habotai Silk Iridescent range by Henry Bertrand, available through Halogen International; jewellery Yellow Door

page 33 sachets in Coral Silk Organza by Henry Bertrand, available through Halogen International; ribbon VV Rouleaux

page 36 Wellington Stripe Cream, Emily Red, Olivia Tea and tied with Basecloth White all Biggie Best

page 37 top: glass bottle House & Interiors

page 38 candles Cotton Gallery

page 39 incense LIM

page 42 bottom left: pots from Prêt-à-pot; garden tools Spirit; top right: Rosebushes wrapped in Chambray

Linen, Biggie Best; top left: model Anniken from Ice Model Management; top Savanna; trousers Juanita Pacheco; garden clogs Saint Verde

page 44 bottom: bags in Basecloth White and Cream and Chambray Linen from Biggie Best; top: floral sachets in Menerbe Bleu and Jaune and St Remy Rouge from Maison Histoire at St Leger & Viney; wooden laminated flooring, Albert Carpets

page 45 heart in White Relaxed Linen from The Studio Collection at Mavromac; blouse Salomé Gunter

page 46-47 soaps and bathballs Fresh; far left: Travel kit sealed by Joypak

page 48 model Amanda James from The Model Company; basin Bright House

page 52 soap dish Prêt-à-pot; sandstone tiles from Just Tiles

page 53 bottles in chill out kit Heals

page 54 model Amanda James from The Model Company; shirt Savanna

page 57 tablecloth in Troyer White Linen from St Leger & Viney far left: Ribbon Paperchase

page 58 Cupboard and chair from Biggie Best; white crockery House & Interiors; table cloth in Troyer White Linen from St Leger & Viney

page 62 bottom right: bubble foil CD package Paperchase

page 63 top: flask Spirit

page 64 model Dale Jackson from Ice Model Management

page 65 cheese knife House & Interiors; ribbon VV Rouleaux

page 66 far right: model Dale Jackson from Ice Model Management; shirt Polo; tie Fabiani; far left: wrapped glasses Fosters; wooden laminated flooring, Albert Carpets

page 68 top left: Cup, teapot and tablecloth House & Interiors; top middle: Infused sugar in glass from Loads of Living

page 69 bottom: Gluwein in glass from Moroccan Warehouse

Suppliers

ABC CARPET AND HOME
888 Broadway
New York, NY 10010
212 473 3000

For other locations contact:
www.abchome.com

*Carpets, linens, fabrics, and a
variety of home furnishings.*

A.I. FRIEDMAN
44 West 18th Street
New York, NY 10011
212 243 9000

For other locations contact:
www.aifriedman.com

*Paper products and other materials,
as well as custom framing.*

BEADS OF PARADISE
16 East 17th Street
New York, NY 10003
212 620 0642

*Many different types of beads
and all the accessories you need to
use them.*

FRESH
2040 North Halstead
Chicago, IL 60614
773 404 9776

For other locations contact:
www.fresh.com

*Bath and body products,
fragrances, and candles.*

IKEA
Elizabeth Center
1000 IKEA Drive
Elizabeth, NJ 07201
908 289 4488

For other locations contact:
www.ikea.com

*Home furnishings, toys, frames,
and other gift ideas.*

KATE'S PAPERIE
561 Broadway
New York, NY 10012
212 941 9816

For other locations contact:
www.katespaperie.com
888 941 9169

Wrapping paper, cards, and ribbon.

KMART
250 West 34th Street
New York, NY 10119-0002
212 760 1188

For other locations contact:
www.kmart.com

*A little bit of everything from
plants and sweets, to tape, glue,
and scissors.*

PEARL PAINT
308 Canal St.
New York, NY 10013
212 431 7932

For other locations contact:
www.pearlpaint.com
1 800 221-6845

*An artist's supply store and much
more, with entire floors devoted to
different media and the widest
selection of colors, materials, and
tools, as well as custom-framing.*

SMITH & HAWKEN
394 West Broadway
New York, NY 10012
212 925 1190

For other locations contact:
www.smithandhawken.com
1 800 940 1170

*A variety of plants and everything
you need for gardening.*

TARGET
North Miami Target
14075 Biscayne Blvd
North Miami Beach,
FL 33181-1629
305 944 5341

For other locations contact:
www.target.com
1 800 800 8800

*Many great gift ideas and all
the supplies you need for
packaging them.*

Acknowledgments

Our special thanks to the brilliant team who have worked together on this book – Robbert Koene, Marlene Wessels, Marina Searle-Tripp, Hermien Coetzee, Jaco Janse van Rensburg, and Emma Wright. We would like to thank all the companies and stores who generously loaned and supplied the products that appear in the book.
A special thanks also to the following for their contribution:
Biggie Best (use of location); Loft Living (use of location); Antoinette and her team (sewing projects); Ellen Fitz-Patrick (copy editing); Isabelle Schreuder (cake icing projects); Bertine Kruger (floral embroidery on linen sachets); Susan Hansen (crochet work – cup warmers and hot water bottle cover); Lille Rall van Eden (handwriting labels and recipes); Anne Taylor (writing poetry on ribbons); Rianne Voigt (herb bundles); Arne and Fransie Frandsen (sourcing and sending requested items from London); Belinda King (creating selected projects); Ronél Palmer (hair and make-up); Leza Marais (sourcing of clothing).
Most of all, thank you to Gerhard, Mia, Ben, and Thinus for their unlimited support.